Praise for *The Indispensable LinkedIn Sales Guide for Financial Advisors*:

A very practical how-to guide for any financial advisor who wants to harness the power of LinkedIn as a sales tool.
— Dave Kerpen, New York Times Bestselling author of *Likeable Social Media, Likeable Business* and the *Art of People*

The strategies shared in this book provides financial advisors with a differentiator when defining their digital presence. This book is a must read for any financial advisor looking to bring in business with LinkedIn.
— Kevin Kozuszek, Marketing and Communications Director, Wells Fargo

As an early adopter of Financial Social Media, I have found the biggest issue is lack of proper education and training. This book does an impressive job in addressing both.
— Mitch Slater

Most advisors have seen and used the investment pyramid that illustrates the farther up the pyramid you travel, the greater the potential reward. Kevin and Matt's insight on social media can be likened to that same theory. Those who accept the challenge and climb to the pinnacle of social networking will reap huge rewards while their less ambitious contemporaries will watch the parade pass them by. Well written, easy to understand, a must read for those who aspire to reach elite status in the advisory business.
— Fred Hensler, CEO, Sapphire Blue Investment Partners

If you are a financial services professional interested in understanding the power of LinkedIn, this book is a must read. Kevin Nichols and Matt Oechsli have provided a roadmap to achieving success using clear and simple steps.
— James M., Financial Advisor

Kevin Nichols is our essential "coach" for incorporating LinkedIn into our practice. His ideas and suggestions are the backbone of our LinkedIn success in meeting new potential clients and growing our practice.
— Michael K., Financial Advisor

As a new financial advisor, LinkedIn has become an essential tool for sourcing new prospects. By utilizing Kevin's and Matt's world class guidance, I have used LinkedIn to not only grow my practice, but become a top acquiring financial advisor in new households and new assets.
     —Jeff S., Financial Advisor

As an advisor who is an avid user of LinkedIn, this is a must have resource.
     —Wealth Management Advisor, San Jose CA

I was very reluctant to join the social media revolution. Kevin and Matt's book gave me practical reasons why I shouldn't be resistant to change and the tools necessary to take a more active and updated marketing approach to acquiring affluent clients. I am excited for what I believe this process can do for me and my practice.
     —Lisa K., Financial Advisor

If you are a financial advisor looking to maximize your networking potential on LinkedIn, then this book is a must read. Matt and Kevin walk you through a process for making the best use of your time on LinkedIn. You especially won't want to miss the 30 minute LinkedIn Routine that shows you exactly what to do on LinkedIn. Put this checklist on your desk, follow it regularly, and engage with your connections like never before. Traditional sales processes are changing and The Indispensable LinkedIn Sales Guide for Financial Advisors will show you step-by-step how to use the world's largest professional social network to position yourself as a knowledge expert to qualified prospects.
     —Adam Zuercher, CPA/PFS, CFP®

"Your Business Will Grow in Direct Relationship to the People You Know", this book will help you grow the number of qualified introductions to prospects you can ascertain. Many of those introductions will become Centers-of-Influence for you and many may become clients. In either case, reading this book and following its recommendations will definitely help you grow your business!
     —Joe Steinberg, CFP®, LOS 21 years

This book is a dynamic, thought provoking, and instrumental must read for anyone looking to expand their practice or business in the most efficient manner in today's digital world.
     —Philip S., Financial Advisor

As an advisor who was "overwhelmed" by the process of "getting it right" for my LinkedIn profile, I turned to Kevin and Matt for help. From beginning to end (with the edits in between), the Oechsli Institute helped me to create a profile that was compelling and uniquely mine. They also taught me the "tricks of the trade" for networking and creating the ideal list of contacts for maximum benefit. Thank you, Thank you, Thank you!
—Douglas M., Financial Advisor

The Indispensable LinkedIn Sales Guide for Financial Advisors

The Indispensable LinkedIn Sales Guide for Financial Advisors

Mastering the Online to Offline Conversion

By Kevin Nichols and Matt Oechsli

Wealth Management Press
9800 Metcalf Ave.
Overland Park, KS 66212

First edition.

©2015 by The Oechsli Institute

Designed and typeset by Sans Serif
Cover design by Olivia Esteban
Printed in the United States of America
ISBN: 978-09895509-1-8

Contents

Message from Matt

My initial reaction when my esteemed colleague Kevin Nichols suggested collaborating on this book was one of trepidation. It wasn't the writing part, as I've written many books over the years; it was the subject matter: LinkedIn social selling. Not really my area of expertise. Kevin's the industry expert on this subject. He's the one who's consulting with the major firms, and traveling around the country conducting LinkedIn social selling workshops for financial advisors.

Yes, I've been in this industry for 36 years and counting, have led numerous research projects on the affluent, elite financial advisors and wealth management teams. Yes, I speak and conduct workshops on these topics around the world. But writing a book on LinkedIn?

Boy was I wrong. Not only has this project been a blast, but also we quickly discovered that combining our areas of expertise created a synergy. My expertise on affluent selling and elite advisors combined with Kevin's social media knowledge and expertise on LinkedIn created a powerful one-two punch, a synergy where $1 + 1 = 5$.

So, if you're serious about acquiring more affluent clients with the help of LinkedIn, this book is for you.

—Matt Oechsli

CHAPTER 1

Why LinkedIn Social Selling?

It is not the strongest of the species that survive, nor the most intelligent, but the one most responsive to change.
— Charles Darwin

Why LinkedIn social selling? Here's why:

- Jerry acquired $18 million in new assets over a two-year period by leveraging his 1st degree connections for targeted personal introductions, offline, to prospects.
- Tom mastered LinkedIn's *Advanced Search* feature to find prospects that were in between jobs. He automated the process to have LinkedIn send him a list of new prospects every week! To date, he and his father have brought in $9 million in new prospects from rollover opportunities sourced on LinkedIn.
- Ron created a LinkedIn group as a resource for employees whose pension was being terminated from a Fortune 100 company. Within a month, and without any promotion, he had nearly 500 members (prospects) join his group.
- Bob used LinkedIn as a way to deepen relationships with CPAs and attorneys by teaching them how to use it. In a few months he tripled the number of referrals he'd been receiving from these professionals.
- Trena combined her monthly seminars for successful women by connecting with all attendees on LinkedIn. This enabled her to

develop relationships and transition a much higher percentage of attendees into clients.

- Erik, a new advisor with hurdles to clear, brought in eight affluent clients in five months using a combination of cold connecting and cold messaging to targeted prospects, and then meeting with them offline.

These are just a handful of the tremendous LinkedIn success stories we've witnessed. All of this was a direct result of advisors using LinkedIn to make personal introductions, conduct advanced searches, create groups, develop relationships, and cold prospect. We will be going in depth with each of these advisors and others in the chapters that follow.

Over the past three years, we've had the privilege of conducting firm-wide social media training with some of the largest outfits in the financial services industry. We've literally coached thousands of advisors, one-on-one, on building their businesses using LinkedIn. We've seen it all—and now <u>we're going to share the tactics, scripts, email templates, and more</u>, that we've coached these advisors to use. We'll even share with you a 30-minute daily routine to systematize the process.

Trifecta of Research

This book is *not* about the "next big thing" in social media marketing. It's *not* about the newest platform or an up-and-coming social network. It's *not* about your kids on Vine, Snapchat, Instagram, or whatever the flavor of the month is. The truth is, new social networks will continue to evolve and sprout up—that's inevitable.

This book is about getting better at using LinkedIn. Period. It's about how to use the largest professional social network to actually grow your business.

This requires understanding the culture and context of the network. It requires developing the instinct, while having a real-time awareness of the protocol of how to interact, when to connect, and when to go after the business opportunities. Those who master the

FIGURE 1: The Trifecta of Research leverages the knowledge gleaned from our three annual reports.

marketing value of LinkedIn will be viewing their peers in the rearview mirror, eating digital dust. Brace yourself, we're about to show you how today's best LinkedIn-using financial advisors (we refer to them as *Influencers*) are doing just that.

This book is also *not* just about social media. Financial advisors we've classified as *Influencers* have been able to blend their understanding of today's affluent investor with emerging technologies. They understand affluent expectations. They know which marketing tactics the affluent respond to most favorably, and how to execute these tactics without coming across as sales-y. It's somewhat counterintuitive, but the more pervasive digital communication becomes—and it's increasing daily—the more the affluent want personal, face-to-face communication with their financial advisors.

To this end, we conduct two parallel research projects annually: one on affluent investors and the other on financial advisors. For the past two years we've added a third research project: financial advisors' use of social media. This has created what we call a *Trifecta of Research* (Fig. 1) that has provided us with a wealth of useful information.

For instance, from this *Trifecta of Research*, we know:

- The #1 way today's affluent investors discover their advisors is through some form of personal introduction.[1]
- The #1 way the industry's elite advisors are acquiring new affluent clients is through personal introductions.[2]

- The #1 way *Influencers* are acquiring new affluent clients using LinkedIn is through personal introductions.[3]

Notice a trend? It's all about word-of-mouth marketing. Great, so why are we talking about social media? Because LinkedIn is a super-powered tool that can blow wide open the number of people you can strategically access using word-of-mouth marketing tactics. The following chapters are our attempt to provide detailed LinkedIn social selling instruction. Much effort has been given to making all of this content as granular as possible, while integrating what we've discovered about the affluent and the top advisors in the financial services industry.

But if we were to break all of this down to its core, it's all about financial advisors learning how to take online connections offline. The secret is being able to uncover a prospect online, build and nurture a relationship, and eventually convert that connection into some form of face-to-face interaction. This is so critical to social selling that we've coined the term *O-2-O Conversion*™—online to offline conversion—and chosen to use it as the subtitle for this book.

Defining Influencer, Affluent, and Elite Advisor

Throughout the book you will see the terms *Influencer, Affluent,* and *Elite Advisor.* They all have specific definitions from each segment of our *Trifecta of Research.*

Influencer

Influencers are advisors who are excellent at using social media—especially LinkedIn. We wanted to be highly selective in segmenting *Influencers* to make certain we were profiling the social media users that others should imitate. We researched 917 financial advisors and winnowed them down to an elite group of users. In order to be deemed an *Influencer,* advisors had to meet all of the following criteria.

1. Used social media regularly
2. Been introduced or referred through social media
3. Researched a client or prospect on social media
4. Posted updates regularly on social media
5. Acquired new business as a result of using social media

We ended up with a group of advisors (8 percent to be exact) who lead the financial services industry in social media use.

Affluent

This segment had to have investable assets of $500,000 or greater, or a household income of at least $250,000. Occasionally, you will find data on those with $1,000,000 or more in investable assets, which will be labeled accordingly.

Elite Advisor

Elite Advisors are those who have acquired five or more million-dollar clients in the past 12 months, lost fewer than three clients, and rate their career satisfaction as "very satisfied."

Compliance

We recognize the importance of adhering to your firm's compliance guidelines, so by all means do so! We also recognize that these guidelines often vary from firm to firm, which is why we've taken an inclusive approach to what we've outlined in these chapters. That means it's your responsibility to adhere to your firm's compliance guidelines. If we happen to be writing about something, let's say posting custom content, that some of you are unable to do, you can read it or skip it, but don't let it bother you. This subject is so fluid, that it seems compliance guidelines are changing on a weekly basis.

There are *Influencers* bringing in new clients through social media at every major firm. So stop blaming your firm if you've yet to score on LinkedIn. Read on and join elite company.

CHAPTER 2

Why the Traditional Sales Cycle is Dying a Slow Painful Death

We are currently not planning on conquering the world.
—Sergey Brin, Google cofounder

Social media and the Internet have changed the traditional sales process. It used to be that, before making a purchase, an affluent consumer would determine a need, ask around, and then contact the product or service provider directly. Much of the information they needed to make a decision was held captive by the sales representative at that company. But today, a prospect is 57 percent through the sales process before even having a conversation with a sales representative.[4]

So, what are buyers doing if they aren't talking to sales representatives in the early stages of the sales process? They are drawing on the vast quantity of information on the Internet; they are trying to qualify the service provider (Fig. 2). There are two critical components to this qualification process: 1) word of mouth, and 2) hyper-research.

1. Word of Mouth
The Oechsli Institute's research identifies the personal introduction as the number one method used by today's *Affluent* to find a financial advisor. Whether from a friend, a colleague, a family member, or another professional, word-of-mouth influence was at work.[1] It is the founda-

FIGURE 2: Research has shown the average prospect no longer relies on a sales representative to make a purchase decision. Source: CEB

tion of the *Affluent* investor's initial search. We also discovered that the source of the information matters; they want the opinion of their immediate network, not the endorsement of a stranger.

2. Hyper-Research

Next, they begin the online investigation process. And this is truly an investigation. According to a study conducted by Google, the average person needs 8.9 sources of online information before making a decision regarding investments.[4] While this number may seem high to most, keep in mind that the affluent are not only profiling you by looking up your LinkedIn profile and company website, they're Googling "typical financial advisor fees," "how to select a financial advisor," and other related queries. They search for any resource necessary to help in their decision-making process. They hyper-research to reduce risk and, quite simply, because they can. The cost of doing this type of research is very low.

Using word-of-mouth and online research, prospects are doing their due diligence ahead of time in an attempt to prequalify potential advisors. This should come as no surprise. Like many of us who shop or do research online, they are simply looking to save time and find the right solution for their needs.

Rather than sit passively on the sidelines during that first 57 percent of the sales process that may seem out of your hands, why not proactively address both due diligence components by leveraging LinkedIn?

For word of mouth on LinkedIn, your ability to see "who knows who" enables you to ask for targeted introductions. Introductions through your network transfer the credibility of your introducer to you. LinkedIn also allows others to see common connections, again, transferring credibility.

LinkedIn can help position you as a knowledge expert during consumers' hyper-research. As the world's largest professional social network, LinkedIn represents your professional persona online. With the proper LinkedIn branding, you can positively influence your prospects' perceptions. Also, by posting helpful content addressing your prospect's needs and concerns, you can demonstrate your expertise on the subject matter.

Oh, we didn't address the "slow painful death" part of this section. The cause of this suffering (and reason for our overdramatic chapter title) is financial advisors resisting change—resisting the social media revolution. Some advisors, not you of course, are convinced that social media is a fad, that it will come and go like selfies and bell-bottoms. We advise these professionals to go back to their fax machines. The fastest growing demographic across all social networks is seniors aged 65 and older.[5] Social is here for good.

Lastly, if you're still thinking your target market isn't here, think again. Our *Affluent* research rates LinkedIn as the top social network the *Affluent* use to connect with their advisors.[1] Also, according to a study by *LinkedIn* and *Cogent Research*, 87 percent of the *Mass-Affluent* ($100,000 to $1,000,000 investable assets) use social media. Out of those, 44 percent engage with financial companies and 34 percent engage with content from financial companies.[6] Your prospects are out there; it's up to you to go turn them into clients.

A Cautionary Note

It's important to keep in mind that as you engage in social media, the key word is social. "Media" are just the tools to help you reach your audience. "Social" is how you engage and build real-world relationships. Those who master social media are really just masters of social selling and building relationships—online and out in the real world. The skillset is the same. The various platforms we call social media (online networks, video, etc.) just enable them to do it on a grander scale.

As with any tool, the more you use social media for relationship management and relationship marketing, the more proficient you will become. Our research shows that 73 percent of *Influencers* saw moderate-to-high business benefit from social media, whereas only 16 percent of non-*Influencers* saw the same.[7] *Influencers* have developed processes and consistency around social media, and they feel the impact on their business. If your plan is to dabble, expect results to match. Success will require your full commitment.

Is a LinkedIn Premium Account Worth it?

While a Basic (free) account is plenty powerful for social selling, there are a few perks that come with a Premium (paid) account.

More search filters: With a Premium account, you get access to additional search filters like *Seniority, Company Size, Interests, Fortune 1000,* and more.

More search results: The Basic version of LinkedIn lets you see 100 profiles for each search, a Premium account lets you see much more.

Saved search alerts: The Basic version of LinkedIn allows you to save three searches for profile-match alerts, a Premium version let's you save a few more.

Full list of *Who's Viewed Your Profile:* A Premium account lets you see the entire list of people who have viewed your profile over the past 90 days (unless they have chosen to remain anonymous).

Ability to send *InMails:* Premium accounts allow you to send a limited number of direct messages to other LinkedIn members who are outside of your network. These are called *InMails.*

Full profiles: A Premium account gains access to additional profile information for 2nd degree and 3rd degree connections.

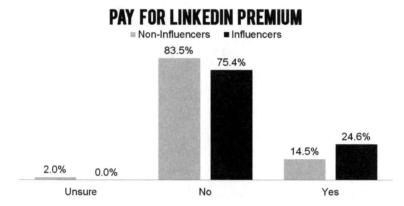

FIGURE 3: Influencers vs. non-Influencers using LinkedIn Premium. Source: Oechsli Institute

Is it worth the upgrade? We think so. But if you aren't convinced right now, that's okay. Currently, 24.6 percent of *Influencers* pay for LinkedIn (Fig. 3), not an overwhelming amount, but we do see this number growing from year to year.[3]

Our suggestion? If you find yourself needing more saved searches, additional filters, or more profile information, a Premium account is worth it. As a publicly traded company focused on generating revenue, it's likely just a matter of time before LinkedIn restricts more and more features to paid accounts.

1st 2nd 3rd Connections, Group Members, Out of Network

Before going any further, we thought it might be helpful to define the various levels of relationships on LinkedIn as they can easily become confusing at times.[8] If you already know this, skip this section.

1st Degree Connections: These are people with whom you are directly connected. You have either accepted their invitations to connect or they have accepted your invitations. You have the ability to send them direct messages through LinkedIn, see their connections (unless they are hidden), and can view their entire profile.

2nd Degree Connections: These are people connected to your 1st degree connections but with whom you are not connected. You can contact 2nd degree connections by asking them to connect, sending them an *InMail,* or asking for an introduction.

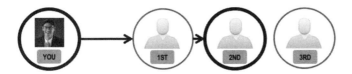

3rd Degree Connections: These are people who are connected to your 2nd degree connections. If their full first and last names are displayed, you will be able to invite them to connect. If only the first initial of their last name is displayed, you cannot connect with them but you can send an *InMail* or request an introduction.

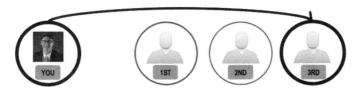

Group Members: These are people with whom you share a group and are considered part of your LinkedIn network. You can contact them by requesting to connect or sending them a message through the group member directory.

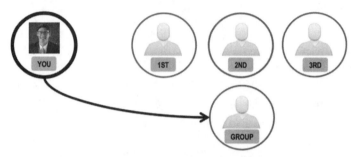

Out of Network: These are people who do not fit any of the previous categories. You can contact them by sending an *InMail.*

CHAPTER 3

Define Your
Ideal Prospect Profile

You have brains in your head. You have feet in your shoes.
You can steer yourself in any direction you choose.

—Dr. Seuss

Attention! Don't skip this chapter. This short chapter is one of the most important in the book.

As we dive into LinkedIn social selling, you need to have a good idea of your *Ideal Prospect Profile*—you need to have a clearly defined target, a direction. Before you read any further, pause and complete the form below. It's imperative that you start thinking of your *Ideal Prospect Profile* in LinkedIn searchable terms. We'll use your answers to the questions below to search for introductions, run advanced searches, find groups to join, post content, and more.

Answer the following questions:

DOES MY IDEAL PROSPECT . . .	EXAMPLE	YOUR ANSWERS
Live in a specific area?	Philadelphia	
Work in a specific industry?	Pharmaceutical	
Work for a large or small company?	Company size of >5,000 employees	
Work for a specific company? Current or past?	Pfizer, Merck	
Have a specific job title? Current or past?	VP, Executive, Director, Global	
Have a certain level of seniority?	VP, CXO	
Have a degree from a specific school?	Thunderbird	
Have a specific certification?	N/A	
Have a shared interest?	Golf, Cycling, Ballet	
Belong to any groups/organizations.	Rotary	
Have certain keywords or phrases on their profile?	Promoted, Retired	

Obviously, most of your prospects are *not* going to meet the answers to all of your criteria, but this is a great starting point. We will leverage your *Ideal Prospect Profile* often, so keep it handy. Also, you may have more than one type of profile—that's a good thing! The more profiles you create, the bigger your prospect net becomes.

CHAPTER 4

Introductions

Knowledge is knowing a tomato is a fruit; wisdom is not putting it in a fruit salad.

> —Miles Kington, author and journalist

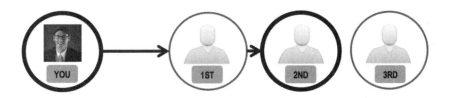

We're going to share Jerry's stories and experiences throughout this section on introductions because this was how he was able to acquire more than $18 million in new assets. But his road to turning LinkedIn into an effective prospecting tool didn't happen overnight. There were many bumps and bruises along the way. It was an entire paradigm shift for him, from personal attitude down to mechanics. Luckily, you can learn from his mistakes and avoid spinning your LinkedIn wheels.

Jerry built the bulk of his advisory business in the 90s using public seminars as his primary marketing vehicle. However, public seminars have run their course, and for the past 10 years he's been struggling to acquire new clients, in particular, clients with affluence. He was frustrated, and looking to find a new marketing strategy that would produce results.

A few years ago, he was introduced to LinkedIn. In fact, he was one of the first advisors provisioned to use LinkedIn at his firm. Excited about the possibilities, he jumped in headfirst and eyes closed. The result? Jerry belly-flopped into the world of social selling and caused a lot of waves in the process.

But less than a year later, Jerry has become an expert. He has mastered the process of using LinkedIn to land personal introductions, to take online connections offline. He has developed a repeatable process and a pipeline that would make most financial advisors envious. But it wasn't an easy process. It took hard work, time, patience, and getting out of his comfort zone.

Why Introductions?

Mastering the personal introduction is essential for any financial advisor interested in acquiring affluent clients in today's world. For the past three years, our *Affluent* research has rated the personal introduction as the number one way the *Affluent* first discovered their primary financial advisors (Table 1). In other words, it's the premier *Affluent* marketing activity for financial advisors to incorporate into their daily routines. Introductions are the backbone for many of the strategies outlined in this book.

Table 1: How Affluent Investors Discovered their Financial Advisor (>$1MM Investable)[9]	
Introduction from friend, family member, or colleague	42%
Introduction from another professional	22%
Other	16%
Community involvement or social activity	6%
Reputation	5%
Public Seminar	3%
Cold Call	3%
Online Research	3%
Direct Mail	1%

Source: Oechsli Institute

Introductions Are NOT Referrals

Let's be clear, asking for an introduction is very different from asking for a referral. Too many advisors see these tactics as one and the same. Our *Affluent* research points out that your clients, prospects, and centers of influence (from here on, COIs) don't like being asked for referrals. They don't like being asked a generic, "Who do you know that I should be talking to?" It's awkward, uncomfortable, and weakens your positioning. Our *Affluent* research shows that eight out of ten *Affluent* investors have a negative reaction to this type of request.[9]

However, a true introduction is quite a different story, especially from the perspective of the *Affluent*. Introductions require knowing precisely whom you would like to meet and asking to meet that person. Introductions require you to do your homework, but the statistics are in your favor:

- 71 percent of *Affluent* investors will introduce you to a specific person if asked (if you have a business and social relationship with them).
- 49 percent will introduce you to a specific person if asked (if you have a purely business relationship).[9]

What makes introductions so powerful is the credibility transfer that occurs when one of your connections introduces you to a prospect. From the perspective of the prospect, it appears that the introducer has identified the transaction as mutually beneficial, transferring a portion of their credibility to you. This is important to realize. You are forcing the hand of word-of-mouth. There is no marketing in the world of the affluent as powerful as the one-on-one introduction.

The best social media-using advisors, *Influencers*, have realized the power of introductions. Our research identified that nearly 83 percent of *Influencers* get introductions through LinkedIn (Fig. 4). Remember, these are the advisors who are actually bringing in business with LinkedIn. Not to mention, nearly 74 percent of *Influencers* get these introductions by asking their client or COI directly—more on this later.[3]

Introductions are the polar opposite of mass marketing tactics. They involve pinpointing specific people you would like to meet and

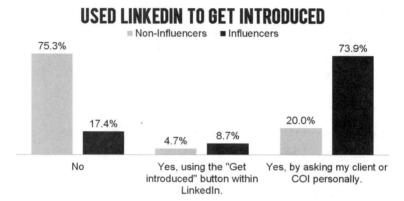

FIGURE 4: Notice a subtle difference in how Influencers land introductions? Source: Oechsli Institute.

asking your mutual connection to introduce you. They require that you invest more time in one person, but this person is someone you've vetted and identified as a potential prospect ahead of time.

> For Jerry, this was an entirely new way of thinking. In the 90s, his seminar approach was to cast a large net and sift through the opportunities. He would mail thousands of people, get a fraction of them to attend his seminar, and then uncover the opportunities within the group, although some were just "plate-lickers" (gross). Jerry had to transition his marketing philosophy from one-to-many to one-to-one. While this approach took some time to master, the results were tremendous.

3 Ways LinkedIn Has Changed the Traditional Introduction

The concept of a personal introduction in marketing is nothing new. But until now, no medium has really impacted this tried-and-true tactic. Thank you LinkedIn! LinkedIn has profoundly changed introductions in three distinct ways.

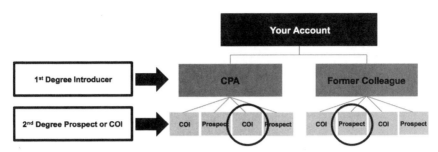

FIGURE 5: LinkedIn's degrees of connection reveal
new layers of potential prospects.

1. Scale

LinkedIn is a powerful resource for uncovering prospects and COIs you may not have known were even in your social sphere (Fig. 5). The introduction playing field just became infinitely larger and more transparent.

2. Intelligence

The amount of intelligence on LinkedIn (and online in general) has never been so vast. You now have the ability to prequalify the people you want to meet. You can see what they do, where they work, where they worked in the past, how long they worked there, and much more. Not to mention, you can also enter into the introduction meeting armed and dangerous with good rapport-building questions.

3. Branding

There is a good chance that your LinkedIn prospects are reviewing your LinkedIn profile before meeting you. You can go ahead and take a look at your profile now if that sentence filled you with panic. This means your prospects are also entering the offline introduction meeting more informed than ever. Fortunately, LinkedIn lets you take control of your digital first impression. There is no reason that your first impression shouldn't be a great one.

Not unlike any other affluent marketing activity, there is more involved than meets the eye of the uninitiated. Invest the time to master our four-step process for LinkedIn introductions and you will thank us for the push.

Phase 1: Be a Giver

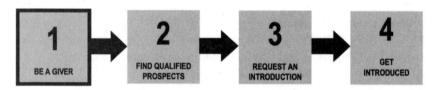

The success of your LinkedIn campaign lies in your ability to build strong and meaningful relationships with the connections that have potential to introduce you. We can't put it more simply than that. Just being connected isn't good enough. You have to develop a healthy relationship with your connections.

The good news is, this is really quite simple. It means activating the law of reciprocity by helping others.

In his gem of a book, *Give and Take*, Adam Grant introduced his readers to a software engineer and entrepreneur named Adam Rifkin. Rifkin was a *Star Trek*-loving computer nerd. Interestingly enough, Rifkin had invested tremendous time and energy into building a massively robust LinkedIn network. A network that would make even Mark Zuckerberg envious—almost. In 2011, Rifkin was named *Fortune Magazine*'s best networker.

As Grant describes him:

> *Rifkin had more LinkedIn connections to the 640 powerful people on Fortune's lists than any human being on the planet. He beat out luminaries like Michael Dell, the billionaire founder of the Dell computer company, and Jeff Weiner, the CEO of LinkedIn. . . . Rifkin built his network by operating as a bona fide giver.*

After creating a successful startup of his own, Rifkin made it his mission to help other startups by connecting entrepreneurs and engineers with business people at larger companies. Rifkin explains the growth of this network in Grant's book: "My network developed little by little, in fact a little every day through small gestures and acts of kindness, over the course of many years . . . with a desire to make better lives of the people I'm connected to."

Grant refers to Rifkin's personality profile as that of a *Giver*. According to Grant, a *Giver* is a person who genuinely gives and looks for ways to be helpful, without expecting an immediate payback. All of his research outlined in *Give and Take* paints a clear picture that *Givers* succeed at the highest levels—they rise to the top.[10] Oh, we should probably mention that Adam Rifkin was so successful he retired in his 30s.

To further reinforce the wondrous law of reciprocity as it pertains to networking, Gary Vaynerchuk, author of numerous bestsellers, speaker, and successful entrepreneur, recently wrote an article for the *Wall Street Journal* discussing his personal secret to networking. He states, "I've learned the true secret to networking is gaining the first-mover's advantage: leverage. The right kind of leverage in a relationship allows you to extract value over time. How does one acquire that kind of leverage? Be the first person in the relationship to provide value."[11]

> Jerry ignored the "be a *Giver*" phase and openly admitted it to us in a coaching session. He said, "I didn't nurture my 1st degree connections enough. I forgot that networking is all about adding value to the other person. I had no leverage and my connections weren't very receptive to introducing me. I probably came across as selfish. It's kind of embarrassing now that I think about it."

There are many ways to position yourself as a *Giver* with your connections. It all boils down to each individual connection and what that particular person values most. Do they value networking support? Small gifts? Information? Time? Your objective is to figure out what your key relationships value, and then deliver. Here are a few ways to become a *Giver*.

Give LinkedIn Introductions

Why not give your clients and COIs exactly what you are requesting? If your connections are actively trying to grow their own businesses, offer to introduce them to others in your network that they may benefit from meeting. From our social media research study we found that 79.7 percent of *Influencers* have offered to introduce one of their LinkedIn connections to another user (Fig. 6).[3]

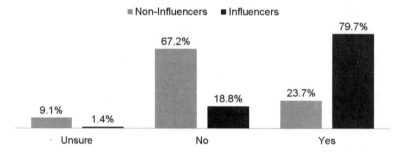

**HAVE OFFERED AN INTRODUCTION
TO A LINKEDIN CONNECTION**

■ Non-Influencers   ■ Influencers

FIGURE 6: Vast majority of Influencers use LinkedIn to help others.
Source: Oechsli Institute.

This can be as simple as saying:

Mrs. Client, I've built a robust network on LinkedIn. I have some peo-ple in my network who can provide expertise in everything from lux-ury travel to renovating your kitchen. If I can ever introduce you, I would be happy to. Just let me know how I can help.

By the way, if the client or COI has children who are about to gradu-ate from college or are job hunting, offer to introduce that child to select members of your LinkedIn network. We've seen multiple advisors do this and the feedback from their clients and COIs has been off the charts.

Give Information

Little things mean a lot in terms of giving. Sending helpful articles and resources is another way to be a *Giver*. Be sure to include a note explaining why you felt it would be pertinent for your connection. The articles don't always have to be business-related. If your connection is interested in gardening or cooking, send an article on those subjects.

> Once Jerry got excited about the concept of being a *Giver*, he came up with a clever and inexpensive technique. Jerry would learn the favorite colleges and professional sports teams of his clients and send them interesting articles pertinent to their teams. At one point, he even had an intern on his team who was responsible for finding the articles. Once he found an article worth acknowledging, he would send the relevant client a personalized email with a link to the article. Sometimes, he would even throw in an occasional joke or competitive jest. His clients loved it and his articles were always a topic of conversation the next time he saw them.

Give Your Social Time

This is appropriate for the 1st degree connections with whom you are interested in building a social relationship. Perhaps they would appreciate you taking them out to dinner or for a round of golf. Investing time to socialize is a great way to develop advocates who are willing to introduce you. Not to mention, our *Affluent* research shows that their willingness to introduce you increases significantly if you maintain business and social relationships. As noted previously, 71 percent of *Affluent* investors are willing to introduce you if you have both a business and a social relationship.[9]

Give Verbal Affirmations

We all love being praised. *Givers* give praise. It's easy to give praise on LinkedIn by liking and making positive comments on your connections' posts. You can also do it in person. If you are in conversation, show that you are truly listening. Most people like to talk about themselves, and want to know they are being heard.

Give Small, Thoughtful Gifts

We call this "Surprise and Delight." Think "coffee table book." What coffee table books would your 1st degree connections like? This forces you to focus on their passions. For instance, if your client or COI is a Chicago Bears fanatic, buy them a book on Mike Ditka. If the COI received an award that was recognized in the newspaper, frame it for them. The gifts should be small, but personalized and thoughtful. The less expensive the gift, the less your motives are questioned.

Our research shows that *Elite Advisors* give Surprise and Delight gifts on a regular basis, with 72 percent claiming to Surprise and Delight top clients yearly or more (Table 2).

Table 2: Elite Advisor Frequency of Surprise and Delight Gifts[2]

Quarterly (or more)	4%
Semi-Annually	14%
Yearly	54%
Less Than Yearly	18%
Never	11%

Source: Oechsli Institute

Develop a strategy to regularly add value to your 1st degree connections in a distinctive way. After all, they are the fastest and most effective gateway to potential new clients. Don't pull a Jerry and skip this step! Your goal is to develop connections who are eager to introduce you to others in their LinkedIn networks. When in doubt, you can always ask your 1st degree connections one key phrase: *How can I help you?* Now that is the mindset of a *Giver*!

Phase 2: Find Qualified Prospects

The next phase for mastering LinkedIn introductions is identifying precisely whom you want to meet. Seems easy right? Think again.

While finding qualified prospects seems simple in theory (peruse your connections' connections), there are important factors to consider.

- **Building a List of *Connectors*:** Your acres of diamonds (new prospects) are hidden behind your best and most highly influential connections. We need to find *Connectors* and leverage them.
- **Filtering Your Connections' Connections:** You only have so much time; it's imperative you know how to search for prospects on LinkedIn in the most time-effective manner.
- **Profile Clues and Activity Clues:** Finding prospects that have good relationships with introducers will increase your request success rate.

Let's break down each factor and find some qualified prospects.

Building a List of *Connectors*

> Jerry liked to ask his LinkedIn connections, "Have you ever set anyone up on a blind date?" While this would often result in a bit of an awkward silence and blank stare from the connection, Jerry was quite serious. From Jerry's perspective, if one of his connections had ever set someone up on a blind date, they are someone who understands networking. That's someone who takes pride in setting people up and creating synergies between others. For this reason, these people were some of the best contacts to approach regarding business introductions. Jerry used this simple (and somewhat goofy) question to help discover the Connectors within his personal network.
>
> He did have one extremely awkward moment however, when he proposed this question to a prominent divorce attorney and she responded, "I thought you were married." She thought Jerry wanted her to set him up on a date. Fortunately, there is a better way to go about finding the Connectors in your network without looking like an adulterer.

Let's face it; some of your 1st degree connections are better at building relationships than others. Some understand LinkedIn networking and some don't. As you venture into the world of LinkedIn introductions, it's a good idea to create a list of *Connectors*.

In his book, *The Tipping Point*, Malcolm Gladwell coined the term *Connector*, referring to people who know lots of people. Gladwell describes *Connectors* as people "with an extraordinary knack of making friends and acquaintances." *Connectors* are people who are experts at cultivating relationships of great depth and breadth. They are also seen as highly influential in their social spheres.[12]

We decided to borrow Gladwell's term, but added some additional criteria of our own. For our purposes, *Connectors* are not only people you know well who are well connected, they are people who are avid LinkedIn users. So take some time to make a list of your personal *Connectors*. We're sure a few names are coming to mind already. Go through your 1st degree connections and answer the following questions to help you build your list.

Is this person connected to my *Ideal Prospect Profile*?

Look through their connections and determine if they are connected to the type of people with whom you would like to work.

Is this person well respected?

They don't have to be Mother Teresa, but they should be respected. *Ixnay* anyone with a slimy reputation. The credibility of the person who can introduce you plays a major factor in the 2nd degree connection valuing the opinion of the introducer.

Think of someone you know who has questionable character. If they messaged or called you offering to introduce you to someone, you would automatically associate these negative feelings with both parties.

Do I have a good relationship and semi-frequent contact with this person?

Connectors with whom you have a personal relationship and frequent contact are going to be more willing and able to introduce you.

Do they pay for LinkedIn?

This is not a must by any means. However, people who pay for LinkedIn are more likely to understand the culture and value of networking.

Do they have more than 50 connections?

The number of connections someone has can tell you a lot about their connection strategy. With 500+ connections, you can be relatively confident that they do not know all of their connections and are less selective when it comes to connecting. With 50 connections, you can be confident they are either extremely selective or don't use LinkedIn much. We find that *Connectors* typically have more connections than the average user.

Not all of these questions have to be answered affirmatively for you to add them to your list of *Connectors*, but use your best judgment when creating your list. Your list of *Connectors* is a gold mine of opportunity and should be treated as such. A concerted effort needs to be made to position yourself as a *Giver* to your *Connectors*. First thing's first—make a list.

Filtering Your Connection's Connections

> Once Jerry had nurtured his list of *Connectors*, he was eager to start finding prospects. Jerry would peruse each individual's connection base on the hunt. But before long, Jerry started to get frustrated. The process of searching through his *Connectors'* connections became a time-consuming and tedious process. If his 1st degree connections had hundreds of their own connections, which many did, Jerry found himself spending hours scrubbing the list for introduction targets. Often he would spend hours researching potential introductions, ask for an introduction, and get an "I don't really know them" response. Frustrating. There had to be a better and more efficient way.

Let's face it, not every person in each *Connector's* network is a qualified prospect. Some have affluence comparable to your connection, others don't. Some are close friends of your *Connector*, and others were met at a business function years ago.

One of the most effective ways to find *qualified* introductions is to search a connection's connections. Thankfully, you don't have to sort through each connection one by one anymore. LinkedIn's robust search capabilities make this an efficient process.

Step 1: Select the *Connector* Who Can Introduce You

This search starts with the advocate in mind. Select the *Connector* who will introduce you. Start with someone who you:

- feel comfortable asking
- believe is connected to others who fit your *Ideal Prospect Profile*
- have positioned yourself as a *Giver* to

This search doesn't have to be done only using *Connectors.* You can use this search on any 1st degree connections that can introduce you. We use *Connectors* because they are your low-hanging fruit.

Step 2: View Their Connections

Locate their connections link, a number toward the top of their profile to the right of the *Send a message* button (Fig. 7). If your introducer's connections are visible, clicking this link will drop you down on their profile to a preview of their connections.

FIGURE 7: How to view a connection's connections. Source: LinkedIn

Step 3: Click on the Magnifying Glass

You will automatically be redirected toward the bottom of their profile where you will see a list of their connections. You could click the *next* button to scroll through 10 of their connections at a time. This is a terribly inefficient way to find prospects. Instead, click on the magnifying glass in the upper right corner of the connections window (Fig. 8), and a text box will appear.

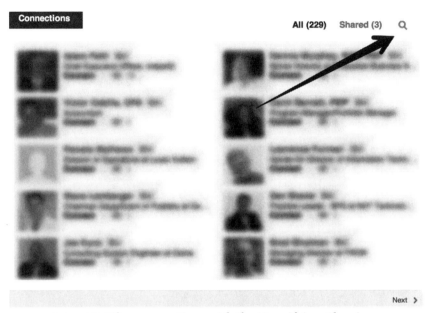

**FIGURE 8: Filter connections with the Magnifying Glass icon.
Source: LinkedIn.**

Step 4: Filter by Keyword and Click on *Advanced Search*

Run a preliminary search by entering a keyword in the text box. Here's where your *Ideal Prospect Profile* comes into play. Is there a particular title, company, phrase, or other keyword your ideal prospect would have on their profile? For example, if you were searching for business owners you might type *president* or *CEO* in the text box. Next, hit *enter* and review your search results. You will now have an *advanced search* option available to you in the upper left corner of your *Connector's* window (Fig. 9).

Step 5: Make Filters Work For You

You can now apply advanced filters on your connection's connections. Refer to your *Ideal Prospect Profile* and layer additional filters on your search. You can narrow your search by *Title, Company, School, Industry,* and more (Fig. 10). Be sure to filter by location, as you will probably want this person to be fairly close in proximity for the face-to-face introduction to take place.

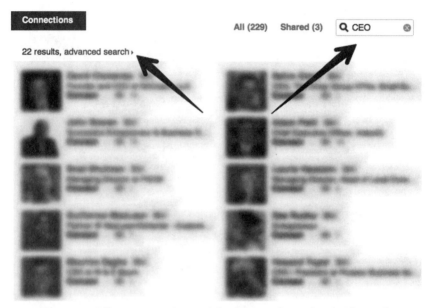

FIGURE 9: Filter connections with a keyword or advanced search.
Source: LinkedIn.

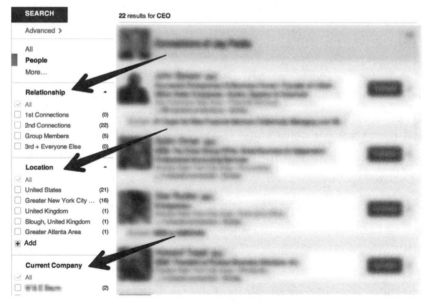

FIGURE 10: Check boxes to apply advanced filters to connections.
Source: LinkedIn.

Searching your connection's connections is a powerful way to build a list of qualified prospects. We'll show you additional ways to uncover qualified prospects by running advanced searches later. For now, this search should keep you busy.

Profile Clues and Activity Clues

So, you've developed a list of *Connectors* and searched your connection's connections. Now you have a list of qualified prospects in front of you. Perfect! Not so fast, there's one more factor we want to consider before requesting an introduction. Your *Connectors* are not always able to provide you with warm introductions to the qualified prospects you uncovered. Your *Connectors* might not even know these people. Ugh! You need some criteria to narrow your focus on high probability introductions.

The following are a few ways to evaluate the relationship between your *Connector* (1st degree connection) and the prospect (2nd degree connection), without ever having a conversation. There are two types of relationship clues we will look for, *profile* and *activity*, and both are equally important.

Profile Clues

Profile Clues include information available on the *Connector's* and prospect's profiles to help you determine areas of commonality.

- Current and Past Employment History: Did the prospect ever work at the same company as your *Connector*?
- Education: Did the prospect go to the same school as your *Connector*?
- Location: Is the prospect in close proximity to you and your *Connector*?
- Groups: Is the prospect in one of the same LinkedIn groups as your *Connector*? Is this a smaller niche group? Is this a national or location-based group?

Activity Clues

Activity Clues give you deeper insight into recent interaction between the Connector and prospect. The more clues you find, the larger the probability a successful introduction will occur.

- Endorsements/Recommendations: Has the prospect recently been endorsed or recommended by your *Connector* or vice versa?
- Recent Connections: Did your *Connector* recently connect with the prospect?
- Engagement: Do the prospect and your *Connector* comment and engage with each other's posts?

As you research qualified prospects, keep these clues in mind. The more profile and activity clues you find between the 1st degree and 2nd degree connection, the better. This means they are more likely to have the type of relationship necessary to make an introduction happen.

Tracking Introductions

> One of Jerry's best practices was to create an Excel spreadsheet of prospects he had sourced through LinkedIn including the 1st degree connection who could introduce him. He would reference this spreadsheet before client reviews or quick impromptu phone conversations with 1st degree connections. He was always armed and dangerous with his prospect list and could easily position the request as an, "Oh, by the way." This spreadsheet was great for requesting introductions in a flash, but it became even more important for keeping track of the process.

As you start sourcing introduction opportunities, your need for a structured way to keep track of your campaign will become evident. Putting the table below in an Excel spreadsheet is our suggested route. We've included columns to help you keep track of basic information (prospect, introducer, profile URL), gauge the relationship between the introducer and prospect (profile and activity clues), and qualify the prospect (qualifying notes).

All of these terms should make sense to you, except for qualifying notes. Qualifying notes are reasons you are targeting this particular prospect. Some of the reasons you want to meet this prospect will be information you listed in your *Ideal Prospect Profile*. Other reasons you want to meet them will be from intelligence you gather while reviewing their profile. As you read numerous LinkedIn profiles, you must develop an eye to find quality prospects. You are on the hunt for things such as:

- Extensive work history
- Multiple high-level job titles
- Looking for a new job (potential rollover)
- Recently retired
- Company went public
- Company is undergoing layoffs

These are just a few examples, but you get the point. Use the qualifying notes column to list the reason(s) you want an introduction to this prospect. At times, you may leverage this information to justify your request to the introducer.

Prospect (2nd Degree Connection)	Introducer (1st Degree Connection)	Prospect LinkedIn URL	Profile Clues	Activity Clues	Qualifying Notes	Status
Tom Reynolds	Jason Lemus	https://www.linkedin.com/in/tomreynolds123	Tom and Jason worked together at Pfizer a few years back.	Jason endorsed Tom. Both graduated from UCLA.	CFO of manufacturing company.	Requested introduction. Jason is reaching out to Tom. I will follow up on 12/1.
Shawn Green	David Sakai	https://www.linkedin.com/in/sgreen67	They both list cycling on their profiles.	David frequently likes Shawn's updates. David wrote a LinkedIn recommendation for Shawn.	Shawn is looking for a job.	Have not requested introduction. Plan to ask during next review meeting on 12/15.

Now you have a list of prospects in hand—nice work. Let's request an introduction.

Phase 3: Request an Introduction

Jerry was a bull in a china shop when he first began asking for LinkedIn introductions. His style (if you want to call it that) was to contact one of his 1st degree connections and say, "I printed a list of 10 of your LinkedIn connections who would make great clients for me. Which ones can you introduce me to?"

Whoa, slow down there eager beaver. At this stage, Adam Grant would classify Jerry as a taker—someone who is only concerned about what they want and doesn't understand the concept of giving.[10] No surprise that this introduction technique didn't work very well. Jerry unwittingly annoyed his connections with his brazen approach. The last thing his affluent connections wanted was Jerry embarrassing them by pitching his services as soon as he was introduced. He had to learn how to subtly sell his connections on personally introducing him, and make them feel comfortable with the process.

This forced Jerry to slow down. He had to determine whether he had become a Giver with his connections first, and then he had to do the necessary homework to qualify the prospects he wanted to meet. Once those two phases were out of the way, he could engage in a general LinkedIn discussion, and seamlessly segue into the LinkedIn introduction request.

Segue into the LinkedIn Conversation

Once you identify people you would like to meet, plan a face-to-face meeting or phone conversation with the person introducing you. Why face-to-face or over the phone? It's more natural and you have an emotional pull. It's easy to ignore an electronic message. As demonstrated

Table 3: Affluent Preferred Communication for Complex Interactions (>$500K Investable)[1]

Face-to-face	71%
Telephone	15%
Email	7%
Combination	7%
Mail	0%
Texting	0%

Source: Oechsli Institute

in Table 3, when it comes to major decisions, the number one preferred medium of communication for today's *Affluent* is face-to-face. Incidentally, the second preferred medium is a personal phone call.[1] You might not realize this, but it is a major decision for affluent clients or COIs to introduce you into their spheres of influence.

Once you're face to face or having a phone conversation, you can easily segue into your introduction request by starting a general LinkedIn conversation. The more you talk with your connections about LinkedIn, the more natural your introduction request becomes. Talking to your connections about their usage helps the *O-2-O Conversion*™. For clients, make it an agenda item during your review meetings. For COIs, continue to be a *Giver* by sharing tips on how to leverage LinkedIn as a prospecting and branding tool. For others, simply ask them about their usage.

Here are some questions to help spark a LinkedIn conversation in general with your 1st degree connections.

- *We're trying to incorporate social media into our business more, in particular LinkedIn. Have you ever used it?*
- *Have you seen this new feature on LinkedIn? I think it's pretty helpful. Can I show it to you?*
- *Do you read LinkedIn Pulse? I noticed an article that might be of interest.*
- *Are you involved in any groups on LinkedIn? I know you went to UCLA. I'm pretty sure there is a large alumni group.*
- *How do you use LinkedIn for business purposes?*

The key is to grease the skids, and then you are ready to ask for a personal introduction.

Finding Your Introduction Request Style

Requesting an introduction can be stressful. You're basically asking for a favor, and no one likes to ask for favors! But the alternative is waiting for a referral—waiting for the prospect (2nd degree connection) to have such a need that they approach your 1st degree connection for advice. Then, we have to assume your 1st degree connection sees you as the go-to source for such expertise and recommends you to the 2nd degree connection. Then, the prospect has to follow through on the suggested advice of your 1st degree connection. That's too many unknown variables for our liking.

We've worked with thousands of advisors on requesting LinkedIn introductions. We've role-played with some top *Influencers*. We've witnessed great success and failure. Through this process, we've found there are some critical components to successful introduction requests.

- **Be you.** If you attempt to use a script that is far outside of your natural style and "not you," you are likely to come across as canned or robotic.

- **Know where your relationship stands.** Tailoring the request to the type of relationship you have with your 1st degree connection is important. The manner in which you ask a friend of 30 years versus a new client is completely different.

- **Have more than one person in mind.** You can't always assume that everyone knows his or her connections well. Identify three to five people you would like to meet through your connection. This increases the likelihood of actually getting an introduction and finding someone the introducer knows well.

- **Inquire about their relationship with the prospect.** It's important that you ask, "How well do you know Mr. Smith and Mrs. Jones?" Asking this question ensures that you don't end up in a dead-end conversation.

A few of our favorite introduction requests are below. You will notice each request has a different style. This is not an end-all list, but it's a great starting point. If you find a style that resonates with you, use it!

The Social-Direct Approach

Jim, I noticed you are connected to Tom Reynolds on LinkedIn. How well do you know him? (WAIT FOR RESPONSE) I would love to meet Tom. What would be the best way for you to introduce me socially?

The Basic Inquiry

Jim, I saw you were connected to a couple people on LinkedIn who look like the type of people we work with. In particular, I noticed Tom Reynolds. How well do you know him? (WAIT FOR RESPONSE) Do you think he's someone I should be talking to?

The Advice Request

I was going to reach out to Tom Reynolds and I noticed you were connected to him on LinkedIn. How well do you know him? (WAIT FOR RESPONSE) I would love your advice on the best way to meet him.

The Ease-In Approach

Jim, I noticed you are connected to Tom Reynolds on LinkedIn. Is he a good guy?

The Correspondence Request

I noticed you're connected to John Smith on LinkedIn. He looks like the type of person we typically work with. How well do you know him? (WAIT FOR RESPONSE) Would you be willing to send him a message on my behalf? (WAIT FOR RESPONSE) If so, I could draft a short correspondence as a starting point for you.

The Gratitude Approach

I know you and Robert Muller are connected on LinkedIn. We're always looking to help people who are a fit for our services. From what it appears, I think Robert might fall in that category. Do you ever run into him? (WAIT FOR RESPONSE) If this comes up in conversation and you're comfortable, I'd be GRATEFUL if you'd tell him that you work with us. We would love to invite him out to lunch.

Survey Leverage

I was reading through the survey we sent out a few months back—thank you for filling that out by the way. You mentioned you would be open to referring us. I happened to look at your LinkedIn connections and noticed a few people who might be a fit for our services. I noticed Tom Reynolds and Lindsay Dawn. How well do you know them? (WAIT FOR RESPONSE) Would you be willing to introduce me to them?

> Once Jerry found his style and wording he was comfortable using, he quickly became a personal introduction machine.
>
> Essentially, Jerry had changed his entire marketing approach. From mass seminars to LinkedIn introductions, it took a huge mental shift. But Jerry made it happen. He was now measuring his marketing by the strength of his relationships and number of personal face-to-face introductions he was able to procure. During an interview, Jerry made an interesting statement. He said:
>
> > *I've found that when I request a LinkedIn introduction, I'm doing more than just asking to meet someone my connection knows. I'm also opening up dialog about introducing me into their spheres of influence. My clients are learning about how I grow my business and the types of people I work with. This conversation is invaluable. I can't tell you how many of my connections start recommending I meet other people they know, beyond the initial person I requested. It's astonishing.*
>
> Within a nine-month period, Jerry brought in more new clients and more assets than he had in the previous three years.

Objections and Stalls

Stalls and objections are part of the game. But don't let these minor speed bumps get in the way of you getting a personal introduction. With a little verbal *jiu-jitsu*, you can easily overcome many of these hurdles and ease any nervousness your 1st degree connection may be feeling. Here are some of the most common objections and stalls you will inevitably encounter and how we recommend you respond.

The 'Keep it Digital' Easy Way Out

A common stall you might encounter is your connection wanting to keep the introduction digital. This is more likely to end in poor introduction results. Your goal is always a face-to-face personal introduction.

Introducer: *I'll send them an email and copy you.* Or *Request an introduction through LinkedIn and I'll forward it along.*

Your Response: *I appreciate that, but I'd really like the opportunity to treat the two of you to coffee or maybe a ballgame, for a more personal connection. You know how these things work. We'll connect on LinkedIn and then it will be difficult to actually meet them.*

If the introducer insists on keeping it digital, that's okay. But try one more time before rolling over and accepting the digital introduction.

The 'Let Me Get Back to You' Delay

Another common stall tactic is your connection letting you know they will talk to the prospect and get back to you. In this situation, you need to put a small dose of accountability on the introducer. If you neglect to put a polite accountability mechanism in place, the request may linger and eventually be forgotten.

Introducer: *Let me check with Mrs. Smith and get back to you.*

Your Response: *That's great. I really appreciate you reaching out to her. I'll give you a call this Friday, after you've had a chance to speak to her, and we can go from there.*

The 'They Already Have a Financial Advisor' Disqualifier

At times your connection will try to disqualify the prospect by letting you know they already have an advisor. Don't let this stop you.

Introducer: *I'm pretty sure they already have a financial advisor.*

Your Response: *That's fine. The majority of my clients had advisors prior to working with me. At this point, I'd just like to meet them socially.*

The 'You Don't Want to Meet Him/Her' Objection

This objection can stop you dead in your tracks if you don't have another prospect in mind. Whether it's intentional or not, your connection is attempting to completely shut down the conversation. Ideally, you want to have a handful of people you've identified, so you are always prepared to throw out another name. That said, if you do get this objection, be ready with your response. Your goal is to thank them for their insight and mention another name. If that doesn't work, ask for permission to continue perusing their LinkedIn connections. You might say:

Introducer: *Oh. You probably don't want to meet John Smith, he's (insert excuse).*

Your Response: *Thank you. I appreciate your insights. I also noticed Larry Johnson. How well do you know him? (WAIT FOR RESPONSE) If I find anyone else you're connected to on LinkedIn who looks interesting, is it okay if I run them by you?*

WARNING: Don't Use LinkedIn's *Get Introduced* Button!

In our latest social media research study, we wanted to know the inner workings of successful LinkedIn introductions. How do advisors actually make successful requests? Do they use LinkedIn's *Get Introduced* feature? Do they send an email? Perhaps they ask via phone? Do they ask face-to-face?

The most startling statistic was that 75.3 percent of non-*Influencers* claim to have never received an introduction through LinkedIn.[3] Come again? LinkedIn is rated the most used social network amongst advi-

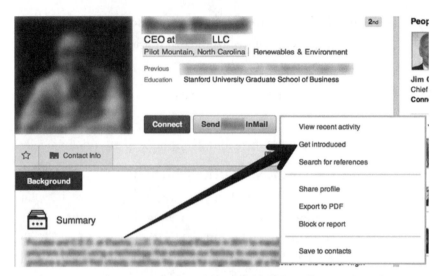

FIGURE 11: The Get Introduced feature (far less effective than direct
communication). Source: LinkedIn.

sors. It also has the highest client acquisition results. So we found this
number surprising; clearly these advisors are missing out.

But when it comes to successful introduction requests, 73.9 percent
of *Influencers* received an introduction by asking their 1st degree connections directly, meaning they had a conversation with a 1st degree
connection about a 2nd degree connection they wanted to meet.[3] They
initiated this conversation face to face or over the phone. Next, they
collaborated with both the client and COI on the best way to make the
introduction happen.

In contrast, only 8.7 percent of *Influencers* successfully received an
introduction using LinkedIn's *Get Introduced* feature (Fig. 11).[3] Thus,
we can conclude that LinkedIn's internal introduction feature is less effective and probably less used than conversing directly with the introducer. We're sure the receptiveness to this feature will grow as social
media receptivity grows, but for now, it's not the best route.

Sure, it's easier to push a button than pick up the phone, engage in
conversation, and make a verbal request. But we also know that you want
results. The technology is just the medium to help pinpoint targets. The
idea is to think less like *Star Trek* and more like *Leave it to Beaver*.

Asking for an Introduction Through Email (Plan B)

Ideally, you have a conversation with your 1st degree connection about being introduced. But there are times when this is not feasible. It might be that your connection is too busy or has not returned your phone calls. Or, they might be at their second home in another part of the country. There are times when reaching them via email might be a viable option.

From our research and coaching, we've discovered some elements that increase the probability of getting a response when you request an introduction through email. Obviously, there is no surefire way to guarantee a response, but including some or all of the elements below can dramatically increase the likelihood of not only a response, but also a personal introduction. Most importantly, you need to convey a sense of both appreciation and importance in the request. Remember, this is *social* media. Don't be too formal in your request. It can run the risk of looking canned and impersonal.

The following are a few key elements that we've seen to opening the introduction door through an email request.

1. **Start with something personal, informal, and brief.**

   It was great seeing you the other night at Printworks Bistro. Your boys are growing up so fast! It sounded like you have some great vacation plans this summer.

2. **Ask for the introduction in a careful and courteous manner—then inquire about the depth of the relationship.**

   I was thinking of you after we met and took a look at your LinkedIn profile. I noticed that you're connected to John Smith, COO of Chevron. If you know him beyond just being connected on LinkedIn, would you be willing to introduce me?

3. **Explain to the introducer why the introduction makes sense—they need to see the logic behind your request.**

   As you know, I really enjoy working with many of the senior executives there and have been able to help them with X, Y, Z.

4. **Give the introducer a few options and then involve them in the process by asking their opinion.**

   If you are open to making a introduction, I'd love to treat the two of you to lunch so I could meet him on a social level. If you think there might be a better way to introduce us, I am open to suggestions.

5. **Give them an out—being too pushy will push them away.**

   If you can't make the introduction, I completely understand.

6. **Mention that you realize you are requesting a big favor and then offer to return the favor.**

   I realize I am asking a huge favor, but if you are able to introduce us, I would really appreciate it. Also, please let me how I can return the favor.

Don't rush your request; be sure to give each step your own unique spin. Remember, it has to have your voice and it needs to be personalized! Your clients and COIs will see right through a copy and paste.

Helping Your 1st Degree Connection Write an Email to Introduce You

> Jerry requested an introduction during a review meeting with one of his top clients, but the client would only agree to send an email to the prospect on Jerry's behalf, and she wanted some help. She asked Jerry to write a script for her. She told Jerry, "Just tell me what to send and I'll send it."

From time to time, the introducer will ask you to script an email correspondence that they can send to the prospect, and it's a great scenario to be in. Your connection is willing to help, but you have to *help* them *help* you.

Sending emails introducing others takes some finesse. In this case, you're scripting someone else which complicates the issue even more. When it comes to describing your services and value, you want to paint a positive picture, but not be too over the top. When you send the email script, encourage the introducer to make any edits or additions. Below is a real-world example we've seen an advisor send a client who wanted to introduce him.

> *To: [Advisor], [Prospect]*
> *From: [Introducer]*
> *Subject: Introducing you two*
>
> *Hi [Advisor] and [Prospect],*
>
> *Hope you are both doing well. I wanted to introduce the two of you, as I think it will be mutually beneficial.*
>
> *[Prospect] – [Advisor] is a great guy and oversees all aspects of our family's financial affairs.*
>
> *He specializes in working with [Insert Niche]. I have worked with him over the last 4–5 years in all aspects of my financial life. You will be hard-pressed to find someone as knowledgeable and personable. I know you will enjoy meeting him.*
>
> *[Advisor]—[Introducer briefly describes Prospect's occupation and their relationship.]*
>
> *I recommend you two find a time to talk on the phone and have [Advisor] explain what he's doing and how he might be able to help.*
>
> *[Prospect], if you are open to meeting [Advisor], can you suggest some times that work for you?*
>
> *Thanks!*
>
> *[Introducer]*

Keep this example handy. It will not only be helpful when scripting your clients and COIs on how to introduce you, it's a good example of how you can send emails to introduce others in your network. Recall, introducing others is a great way to position yourself as a *Giver*.

So now that your 1st degree connection is willing to introduce you, let's knock the introduction meeting out of the park.

Phase 4: Get Introduced

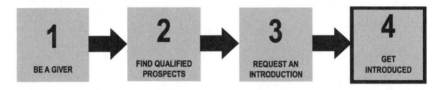

Using Charlie Munger's concept of learning through inversion, Jerry's initial attempts at the *O-2-O Conversion*™ provide a textbook case of what not to do.

When one of Jerry's *Connectors* agreed to introduce him to a mover and shaker in his community, he was blown away. Blown away to the extent that he failed to do his homework. Jerry did no research on the mover and shaker he was about to meet—he just knew the guy had money and was very influential in town. This research is crucial. It's where you find out bits and pieces of personal information that you can use to easily establish rapport. For instance, if a quick Google search uncovers that your prospect has three children and is a member of a local country club, you can ask questions about family or golf. Either way, you are better equipped to get your prospect talking about him or herself, which is an essential ingredient to establishing rapport. By not doing his research, Jerry had made it more difficult to develop rapport.

Jerry then compounded his first mistake by assuming this introduction was his invitation to initiate a business discussion. Without realizing it, his first impression, which is always the lasting impression, was that of a sleazy car salesman. Jerry even brought multiple brochures and his pitch book to the meeting! No surprise, he was unable to get a follow-up meeting with the prospect, and his client began to question him regarding any future connections he wanted to make.

Jerry's coach was able to use his first LinkedIn introduction experience as a teachable moment. So before he began his second online to offline introduction, with a different client and different prospect, Jerry did his research and didn't discuss business. But he did fall into a common affluent sales trap—he talked way too much. Although he didn't annoy his client as much as his first *O-2-O Conversion*™, he wasn't able to transition that introduction into a client.

Jerry is coachable. He learned from his first two forays into online to offline interactions. He realized that without mastering the art of affluent sales, LinkedIn was going to be a black hole, not an end-all-be-all magic marketing tool. Jerry committed to conducting diligent research in advance of each personal introduction. He then reviewed everything with his coach, and they role-played the first personal introduction meeting. And from there it was all about developing a personal relationship and understanding the timing of when and how to segue into a business conversation.

So now you have an introduction meeting lined up. Your 1st degree connection is personally introducing you to a 2nd degree connection, a prospect you've prequalified and would like to meet. This might be happening over coffee, lunch, sporting event, or any other common venue. The objective is for this introduction to be a face-to-face encounter.

It's important that you do not approach this meeting feeling like you must prove yourself. Remember, you have word-of-mouth marketing in your favor. The simple fact that you are being introduced gives you credibility. Today's affluent will not introduce someone into their spheres of influence if they wouldn't recommend their professional services. This is why personal introductions are the most powerful marketing force on the planet. So approach your meeting with the utmost confidence.

Do Your Research

You're getting an introduction through LinkedIn, so start there. Review your prospect's profile and be on the hunt for commonalities. Also, make sure you search through other social networks to see what information you can gather.

Build Rapport

Your main objective is to build rapport with your prospect. Set your business hat aside and focus on sincerely getting to know the person you are being introduced to. Jumping into business right away will be off-putting to both your prospect and 1st degree connection who is introducing you. You always want to put the focus on your prospect—not yourself.

In Table 4 below, you'll see the top three sales turnoffs for *Affluent* men and women. Keep these in mind as you interact with prospects.

Table 4: Sales Turnoffs[1]			
Affluent Female (>$500K Investable)		Affluent Male (>$500K Investable)	
Too Pushy	44%	Too Pushy	30%
Lack of Knowledge	22%	Lack of Knowledge	18%
Talks too much	9%	Talks too much	11%

Source: Oechsli Institute

Dress for Success

Our *Affluent* research is clear on this topic—appearance matters. Your attire matters. Appearance can make or break your first impression, which can make or break your ability to clinch a business relationship. We asked *Affluent* investors how important a salesperson's dress was in our latest study (Table 5).

Table 5: Importance of Salesperson Dress (> $500K Investable)[1]	
Not at all important	2%
Slightly important	18%
Neutral	14%
Moderately + Extremely important	67%

Source: Oechsli Institute

3 Paths for Follow-Up

Approach your initial introduction meeting with the appropriate expectations. You are meeting someone new. Your goal is to start building a relationship, not to get them signing paperwork. As for next steps, there are a few possible paths your introduction meeting might take:

1. **Purely Social.** If your prospect never gives you an opening to segue into business, that's okay! Let the conversation be social, and look for ways to follow up socially. What are their passions? Golf? Baseball? Cooking? Fine dining? Use the information you uncover to arrange a social point of contact in the future. Whether it's a lunch to share LinkedIn connections, a round of golf, or some other non-business interaction.

2. **Purely Business.** If the conversation takes a business tone—great! Your objective is to schedule a business follow-up meeting with your prospect. Depending upon the tone of the conversation, determine if they should come directly to your office or if a business lunch might be more appropriate. At times, your client or COI, the introducer will prompt a business conversation and that's a good thing.

3. **Redirect Opportunity.** Redirecting a conversation is basically verbal *jiu-jitsu*. It's taking a conversation about the economy, markets, political environment and more, and turning it into what you are doing for your clients. You can then prompt a question to your prospect regarding business. This is a high-level affluent sales skill and will take time to master. Here is an example:

If your prospect is complaining about the uncertainty in the markets, you might redirect the conversation by saying:

I could see how you would feel that way. We're working closely with our clients making sure they're protected and taking advantage of any opportunities we can find. Would you be open to meeting and making sure you're protected as well?

You can redirect endless conversations if you are prepared. The key with personal off-line introductions is to come out of your initial meeting with a clear follow-up game plan. Your objective is to leave knowing which of the three paths you will take your prospect down.

Other Follow-Up Touches

You just left your initial introduction meeting. You had a great conversation and uncovered a lot of personal intelligence—passions, hobbies, interests, and more. You know which of the three paths you are going to take your prospect down. You're back at the office, so now what? The secret is to blend your digital outreach with an old-school personal touch. Here are some ideas on ways to create additional touch points with prospects.

- **Connect on LinkedIn**
  Well of course! If you haven't already, send a personalized invitation to connect on LinkedIn immediately after the meeting.

- **Follow Them on Twitter**
  It may be too soon and too personal to connect on Facebook. However, if the prospect has a Twitter account you should follow them. This will keep you abreast of any other updates in their life.

- **Offer to Introduce Them**
  If you are connected to others they might benefit from meeting, offer to introduce them.

- **Send a Thank You Note**
  While this might seem dated, it's a nice personalized touch, and rare nowadays. Take the time to write something personal. The note doesn't need to say anything more than the following:

  I enjoyed meeting with you and (introducer) over lunch at (name of restaurant) this past Tuesday, let's stay in touch.

- **Send an Article on a Personal Interest**
  You want to position yourself as a *Giver*. Think back to your con-

versation and identify any passion points you uncovered. Take these passions points and find a pertinent article to send as a touch point. For example, if they like vegan cooking, see if you can find articles or recipes online to send.

Introductions: Your LinkedIn Routine

From here on, at the end of each chapter, we will suggest action steps that could become part of your LinkedIn routine.

ACTION STEPS TO CONSIDER:

1. Position yourself as a *Giver* with *Connectors* and other 1st degree connections with introduction potential. Determine what the connection values most and deliver. This may be providing them with an introduction, sending a helpful article, or delivering a Surprise and Delight gift.
2. Pinpoint multiple introduction opportunities to prospects weekly. Leverage your *Connectors*, search their connections, and keep in mind *profile* and *activity* clues.
3. Ask for a LinkedIn introduction; execute an *O-2-O Conversion*™ a few times per week. This is a numbers game. Ideally, make this introduction request face to face or over the phone.

CHAPTER 5

Your Network

I'm so shy I make Bigfoot look like a socialite.
—Jarod Kintz, author of *Emails from a Mad Man*

Trena came from a background in the apparel industry. She was the VP of Sales for her former employer and had done quite well for herself. But when her company was purchased, she soon found herself searching for another career and ultimately landed herself a job as a financial advisor with a major firm. Using the same networking skills that helped her climb the proverbial corporate ladder, she embarked on a new adventure.

Trena would never consider herself tech savvy, but she understood the networking aspect of social media and diligently built a network using LinkedIn. This LinkedIn network contributed to her growth from a rookie with no clients to a very successful advisor, more than she could have ever expected.

There is no question that Trena's corporate experience and contacts were helpful in launching her career, but she also did a lot of things right when it came to building her LinkedIn network. We're going to share with you some of Trena's philosophies and techniques in this section on building and cultivating a powerful network.

Quality or Quantity or Both?

The network you build on LinkedIn will be one of your biggest business assets going forward. But what makes a strong LinkedIn network? Is it the number of connections? Or is it the quality of the connections you've made?

We've all considered the question of quality versus quantity at some point. Whether we accepted a LinkedIn request from someone we didn't know, or we followed numerous people on Twitter hoping that they would follow us back. We've all experienced these crossroads.

The truth is, there are arguments for both quantity and quality and there is no shortage of opinions in this debate. Larger networks allow you to reach more people, generate more awareness, and create perceived credibility. If I have 1,500 connections, I must be good, right? Quality networks increase engagement, improve search results, and ultimately raise conversion rates. In reality, both the breadth and depth of your network matters. Elements of both quality and quantity are necessary for any successful social media strategy. Having a network of 10 quality connections will not get you far. But having 10,000 connections with no interest in you also will not catapult your career.

We decided to put this debate to the test in our social media research project. We asked advisors how selective they are when deciding to connect with someone on a social network. Our research uncovered that *Influencers* are more selective (53 percent versus 35 percent) of who they connect with through social media.[13] Thus, *Influencers* favor the quality argument (Fig. 12).

> Trena wisely opted for quality, and developed a simple way to make a decision about who to connect with. In an interview she said:
>
> *My litmus test for connecting with someone is if they would return my phone call. If they wouldn't, I don't connect. I want a network of people who can really help me grow my business. Plus, I want to be able to offer and receive introductions. I can't really do that if I don't know my connections well. Nothing is more frustrating to me than running an advanced search for prospects (2nd degree*

> connections), finding someone I want to meet, and finding out that
> I don't really know the person who can introduce me (1st degree
> connection). How can I ask someone I don't know to make an
> introduction?

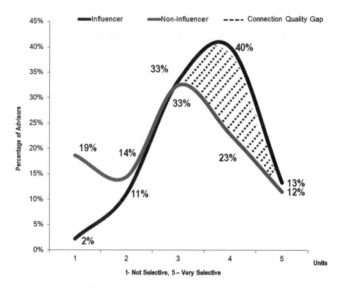

**FIGURE 12: Influencers are choosy when it comes to connecting.
Source: Oechsli Institute.**

Our coaching of advisors on social media, combined with our *Trifecta of Research*, push us toward a strategy of building quality connections. However, that does not mean you should dwell within the comfort bubble of your quality connections. You must use your quality connections to build more quality connections!

Building Your 'Tribe'

LinkedIn is the perfect tool to collect your most important relationships, all in one place. Building your network is a fluid process—it should never stop. When building your "tribe," here are the types of connections we recommend you add to your network.

People you <u>know well</u>

This consists of both personal and professional people you know. It includes good clients, COIs, former colleagues, friends, and family members. You'll want to make a list of all of these people and then search for them on LinkedIn. You can do this individually by typing each name in the search bar at the top (Fig. 13). If they have a generic name, you may need to add additional details to your search to narrow your results. For example, you might want to include a company, title, or location.

1 result for **Bob Muller Raytheon**

FIGURE 13: **Manually search for people you know IRL at the top of the page.**
Source: LinkedIn.

> Trena was diligent in building her connection base. After all, she had no time to waste. She started by importing contacts from her personal email into LinkedIn. That said, she didn't invite everyone from her email list. She selectively unchecked the invitation box next to people with whom she didn't want to connect. She also posted a message on Facebook asking her other good friends to connect with her on LinkedIn. Lastly, she used the *People You May Know* feature daily (more on this later). She built a large and quality network in a matter of weeks.

People you've met and <u>want to know well</u>

These are people you've met in person, you don't really know personally, but with whom you'd like to develop a deeper relationship. Some might call these superficial connections. It includes people who could be prospects, networking contacts, and the children of your clients. By adding these people to your network, you are combining your real world networking with online networking. The idea here is to make sure you never miss an opportunity to connect.

> Trena had a robust list of people she needed to know better. She increased contact and focused on developing more personal relationships with each. Trena also reconnected with past relationships, including fellow alumni. As a graduate from Virginia Tech, there was a robust network of alumni on LinkedIn. Trena was able to find them using the *Find Alumni* feature. She found people she had completely forgotten about, including an old roommate.

You will definitely want to take advantage of the *Find Alumni* search on LinkedIn (Fig. 14). This allows you to search universities to find a list of professionals who went to school when you did. Find out what these people are up to now, connect on LinkedIn, and rekindle dormant relationships.

FIGURE 14: **Find Alumni function is a powerful tool. Source: LinkedIn.**

People you would <u>like to meet</u>

You will also stumble upon people you would like to meet on LinkedIn. Here is where you want to be careful. Avoid requesting to connect to multiple people you don't know. If you are actively searching for people you would like to meet and find someone, focus on getting personally introduced offline through a mutual connection if possible.

People you've met <u>who love LinkedIn</u>

You'll find certain people use LinkedIn more than others. You definitely want to connect with other avid users like yourself. These people are often open to introducing you to their connections, and they understand the culture of LinkedIn, so you can learn from each other.

Don't Build a Network of Competitors (Other Financial Advisors)

For most advisors, your tribe should not consist of other advisors (competitors). We see this mistake often. Ask yourself the following questions before connecting with a competitor.

- Is this person going to give me introductions to prospects?
- Am I comfortable giving this person access to my clients and COIs?

If you answered "yes" to both questions then please, ignore our advice. But for the majority of financial advisors, connecting with other advisors is not a good idea. Our advice is you simply ignore their requests.

Types of Connections to Consider

As you rack your brain to recall people you would like to connect with on LinkedIn, consider the list below. While this list is incomplete, it should help jog your memory and recall people you could have easily forgotten about.

- Clients
- Prospects
- CPAs
- Estate attorneys
- Current friends
- Past friends
- Former colleagues
- Religious affiliations
- Board members
- Neighbors
- Golf/tennis friends
- Fraternity/sorority contacts
- Committee members
- Alumni group members
- Parents of your children's friends

You'll most likely be surprised at how quickly you can build your LinkedIn "tribe" if you devote some serious time to it.

Personalize Invitation Requests

No matter who you request to connect, you should always personalize your invitation. It's good LinkedIn etiquette. Don't use the standard LinkedIn language. Personalizing your request starts the relationship off on the right foot. It shows your potential connection that they are worth the time and it gives you an opportunity to be a *Giver* right away. If your new connection would benefit from meeting people in your network, offer it up at the end of your request. Also, keep it social and light! This is a *social* network. Here is an example:

> *Bob,*
>
> *Nice seeing you the other night at Green Valley Grill. It was great catching up. It's hard to believe Mitch will be headed to college already!*
>
> *We'll have to catch a Virginia Tech game this year.*
>
> *I would love to add you to my LinkedIn network, and if I can ever introduce you to any of my connections, just ask.*
>
> *—Trena*

People You May Know

Take advantage of the *People You May Know* feature on LinkedIn. It's an easy way to discover people you met in a former life and totally forgot about. LinkedIn's algorithm for determining the list of suggested connections is amazing, even scary accurate at times. As you build your connection base, you will want to use this feature daily. When on your home screen, it's located in the upper right hand corner (Fig. 15).

People You May Know

_____ Director of
Operations and Business
● Connect

_____ Wealth Advisor -
Raymond James Financial
● Connect

_____ Senior
Director, Credit Policy
● Connect

See more »

FIGURE 15: People You May Know is an eerily accurate, automated feature in the upper right hand corner of your home screen. Source: LinkedIn.

Connection Requests from Strangers

Whenever you get a connection request from someone you don't recognize, it's time to do some detective work. You need to uncover the intent behind the invitation to connect. Here are the most common reasons someone might ask to randomly connect. We've also given our basic recommendation on whether or not to accept their connection request:

- They are a LION. This stands for LinkedIn Open Networker. These people connect with anyone and everyone to build massive LinkedIn networks. Some do this to get access to your email address and then send you emails (spam). Unless you are implementing a cold connection strategy (more on this later), don't connect.
- They want to sell you something. Unless you want what they are selling, don't connect.
- They see potential to do business with you or create a synergy. Definitely connect with this person.
- They have met you and you don't recall. Ask this person when and where you met and then decide if you want to connect.
- It has been suggested to them by one of your 1st degree connec-

tions that you'd be a good person to connect with. In social media parlance, this is an *indirect referral.* Definitely connect with this person.

So what's the best way to uncover this person's intent and how should you respond? Simply ask, but do this in a candid and inoffensive way. You can reply to their invitation to connect without accepting (Fig. 16).

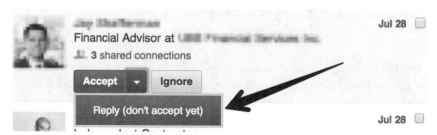

FIGURE 16: Don't jump the gun! Consider contacting a potential connection before ignoring or accepting an invite. Source: LinkedIn.

Trena was proactive about increasing her connections and never left a stone unturned. By that, we mean that whenever she received an invitation to connect from someone she didn't know, she didn't ignore the request (which some advisors do), rather she would respond with a simple question, *Have we met?*

From that simple question, Trena uncovered people who had been referred to her, using LinkedIn as the medium. Because she was so active in building her tribe and staying in touch with her connections, her clients and COIs frequently referred people to Trena who she didn't know. Also, the great content she spread through social media often led prospects to her, prompting a request to connect.

It's that simple. If you are focused on building quality connections on LinkedIn, don't be afraid to ask someone about their intent before accepting their invitation. After all, they are the one with the poor LinkedIn etiquette.

How to Disconnect

Years ago, when advisors initially created their LinkedIn accounts, many were liberal when it came to connections. They accepted requests from anyone and everyone. This included competitors, shallow acquaintances, recruiters, sales people, and more.

Here's your reality: if you have undesired connections or feel you are being spammed, you can and should disconnect. Here are some facts, straight from LinkedIn, that you should be aware of when you disconnect from someone[14]:

- When you remove a connection, they won't be notified.
- After removing a connection, any recommendations or endorsements between you and that person will be withdrawn. They will not be added back if the connection is re-established.
- Only the member who breaks the connection can reinitiate that connection.

Removing connections is a simple process. Start by clicking on the *Connections* link at the top of your screen. Scroll through your connections and find the person with whom you would like to disconnect (Fig. 17). Hover over their name and select the *More* option. Lastly, select *Remove connection.*

FIGURE 17: The old heave-ho. LinkedIn makes it easy to disconnect.
Source: LinkedIn.

How to Power Up Your Network

So now you have a solid number of LinkedIn connections and you've avoided connecting with competitors. Now you're ready to power up your network.

According to British anthropologist Robin Dunbar, the neocortex of the brain is built to sustain a social network of around 150 people. Beyond 150, we just aren't cognitively capable of keeping track and building personal relationships with people easily.[15] If our ability to maintain relationships is limited, we need to do a better job of managing the strength of our network and focusing on the right types of people.

Using two variables, frequency of contact and personal relationship, we've developed a way for you to easily segment your existing connections (Fig. 18). Through this segmentation process, you can gauge the strength of your existing network and determine the best course of action to help you build a strong and prosperous one.

Most of the contacts in your network fall into one of four categories:

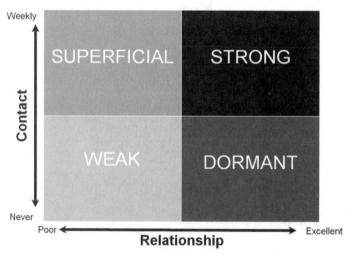

FIGURE 18: Start by rating the strength of your network.

So what does your network look like? For most financial advisors, it's a blend of the above categories. After you segment your own network, here are a few tips on how to power up each category:

Strong Connections

These are people you know personally and see regularly. *Connectors* typically fall into this category. Your objective is to build a network rife with strong connections. Nourish this group and leverage them for introductions to prospects and COIs. Make certain that you're a *Giver*, as you never want to be perceived as abusing these connections. It may be tempting to approach them regarding business on a regular basis, but do this sparingly.

Dormant Connections

These are people you knew well in the past, but with whom you no longer associate. This might be an old colleague, friend from college, or former COI. To transition this segment into strong connections, devise a plan to increase your contact and rekindle the relationship. Remember, position yourself as a *Giver*.

According to Adam Grant, dormant ties often present a large opportunity for networkers and sales professionals. Why? You already have an established relationship with them and they typically have additional ties and relationships of which you are unaware. They present a fresh network that has yet to be harvested.[10]

Superficial Connections

Superficial connections are people with whom you have regular contact but a shallow relationship. These are people with whom you exchange pleasantries at networking events but don't take out to a private dinner. Also, these could also be people you've never met in person, but interact with online. To transition these connections from superficial to strong, you need to develop a deeper connection. Get to know them personally, be a *Giver*, and then schedule some offline one-on-one personal contact in a different environment. Coffee anyone?

Weak Connections

If there is no opportunity, no commonalities, no personal relationship, and no desire to nurture—disconnect. Weak connections take the most energy to develop into strong connections. They require more contact and more personal relationship development. Determine which connections you are willing to nourish and which ones you plan to jettison. Only connections that could offer business opportunities in the future are likely worth the time and effort.

Let's be very clear about this—your ability to bring in business with LinkedIn is contingent upon the quality of your network. Take your LinkedIn network seriously; your future business depends upon it.

1st Degree Connection Audit

Before you finish this chapter, it's time to run an audit on your connections. We need to gauge the quality. This can often be quite eye-opening for advisors.

For each of your connections, give a *Contact Frequency* score and a *Relationship* score. This is not an exact science, but do your best to gauge your relationships with your 1st degree connections and plot your results on the model below. We included a few examples.

1st Degree Connection	Relationship 1 – Poor 2 – Fair 3 – Good 4 – Very Good 5 – Excellent	Contact Frequency 1 – Never 2 – Annually 3 – Quarterly 4 – Monthly 5 – Weekly	Category Strong Dormant Superficial Weak
Jay	5	1	Dormant
Ryan	2	2	Superficial/Weak
Rory	4	5	Strong
Jim	1	2	Weak

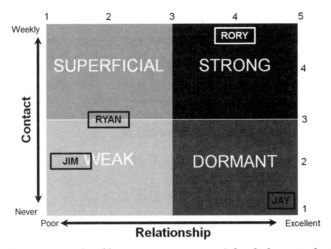

FIGURE 19: **An example of how your contacts might shake out when rating. Goodbye Jim, Hello Rory!**

What were your results? Do you have a mostly dormant network? Do you have plenty of strong connections? Now you have to develop a game plan to boost your connections to the strong category. In the example we used, we would increase contact with Jay, build a more personal relationship with Ryan, and if we had no desire to cultivate Jim, we would disconnect. Oh, and Rory is someone we should be leveraging *now!* (Fig. 19)

Your Network: Your LinkedIn Routine

We've learned a lot about developing a connection strategy in this section. Below are some suggested action steps.

ACTION STEPS TO CONSIDER:

- Think back to people you've met recently and send them requests to connect on LinkedIn. Make sure you personalize each request.
- Review the *People You May Know* feature on LinkedIn to identify long lost contacts.
- Identify one superficial or dormant connection daily and make an effort to transition them to the strong category. For example, with a superficial connection you may be scheduling a one-on-one lunch to get to know them personally. And for a dormant connection you may be catching up with a phone call to rekindle the relationship.

CHAPTER **6**

Advanced Search

We've all heard that a million monkeys banging on a million typewriters will eventually reproduce the entire works of Shakespeare. Now, thanks to the Internet, we know this is not true.

—Robert Wilensky, artificial intelligence expert

Tom joined his father's practice in Philadelphia eight years ago as his succession plan. As Tom's father was phasing out, Tom realized his father had prepared him well in running the business, but when it came to client acquisition, he felt lost. Their client base was getting older and the business was slowly constricting.

After Tom saw one of our webinars, he decided to give LinkedIn a try. Tom grew up with social networks and was very comfortable with the technology side of things. He was a computer science major in college. It just seemed natural that he would utilize LinkedIn to discover opportunities. And he became really good at it. In this section we'll share a few of Tom's search techniques and embarrassing bloopers.

LinkedIn's *Advanced Search* function is powerful. Think of it as a souped-up Corvette. It can take you wherever you want to go, and it can get you there at breakneck speeds. The irony is that most advisors drive this Corvette like a grandmother. They never take it out of second gear! They poke along and cling to the wheel. Well, we're going to show you how to take LinkedIn's *Advanced Search* feature out on the highway and really open it up. Buckle up—you're about to get a speeding ticket.

Our research indicates that *Influencers* run multiple types of advanced searches (Fig. 20). From finding COIs, executives, business owners and money in motion—they do it all.[3] In this chapter, we will show you how to run some of the most essential searches for financial advisors. Remember when we encouraged you to create an *Ideal Prospect Profile*? This is the section where it will be the most useful. So pull it out and keep it handy. You should input terms from your *Ideal Prospect Profile* into these searches to make them more pertinent to you.

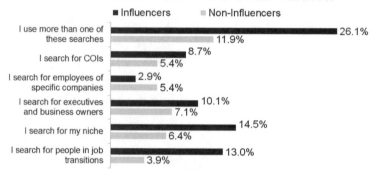

USAGE OF LINKEDIN ADVANCED SEARCH

FIGURE 20: **Influencers are more active and creative with Advanced Search. Source: Oechsli Institute.**

Anonymous Mode

We all have embarrassing moments in life, and one of Tom's was in the locker room at his club's golf course. "Hey Tom, what are you, one of those cyber stalkers? I always see you looking at my LinkedIn profile," one of the members shouted from across the locker room. The accusation couldn't have been more awkward. Tom mumbled a response that he was doing a little research on LinkedIn and its usage amongst members, but he knew he'd been busted. Tom had neglected to go into Anonymous Mode on LinkedIn prior to conducting his searches—he didn't know it was an option. Trust us, Tom never made this mistake again. No one forgets being accused of being a stalker in a men's locker room. No one.

If you are planning to do some serious LinkedIn prospecting or re-search, it's always a smart move to switch your profile to anonymous. By default, LinkedIn will show you who has viewed your profile, and vice versa. So if you'd prefer *not* to let someone know you have been re-searching them, it's important to change your settings. LinkedIn lets you become anonymous with the click of a button.

Here are some times you might consider going into anonymous mode. When you are:

- Meeting a prospect you are not connected with and want to gather some information from their profile
- Running advanced searches to pinpoint your target market
- Running a connections' connections search
- Conducting competitive intelligence

To change your visibility settings, go into *Privacy and Settings* and click on the link labeled *Select what others see when you've viewed their profile* (Fig. 21). You will then have three visibility options. Select *You will be totally anonymous.* Success! You're now in anonymous/stealth/stalker mode!

After you've completed your investigation, make sure you remember to revert back to your original setting. Turning on the anonymous feature will disable your ability to see who has viewed your profile with the free version of LinkedIn. The only way to stay in anonymous mode

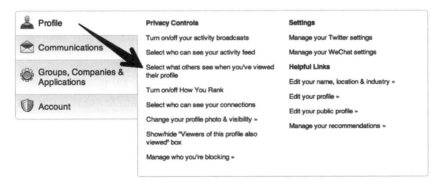

FIGURE 21: **Time to go incognito. View users' profiles without notifying them. Source: LinkedIn.**

and still see who viewed your profile is to upgrade to a Premium account.

Boolean Logic

Before we dive into searches that can help you build prospect lists, let's briefly discuss how these searches are conducted. We will be combining the *Advanced Search* fields with Boolean modifiers. Boolean logic was named after 19th century mathematician George Boole. It's basically a form of algebra in which values are reduced to TRUE or FALSE. It may seem like nerd-speak but it's actually super easy to learn and will greatly improve the accuracy of your LinkedIn *Advanced Search* results. Boolean logic is like adding a turbocharger to your Corvette.

Boolean search uses specific modifiers (quotes, parenthesis, AND, OR, NOT) to help you find the LinkedIn users you are looking for. You are basically building search strings. You can build Boolean search strings in the following fields within the *Advanced Search* section on LinkedIn.

- *Keywords*
- *Title*
- *Name*
- *Company*

Quotes
If you are searching for an exact phrase, enclose the phrase in quotes.

- "Vice President"
- "sold my practice"

Parenthetical
If you would like to combine certain terms and modifiers, use parentheses. Parentheses require that the terms inside of them be searched first.

- Software AND (engineer OR architect)
- Pfizer AND (president OR executive)

AND (ALL CAPS)

This modifier narrows your results. Use this when you want to insist that two or more terms be on someone's profile.

- software AND engineer
- VP AND Raytheon

OR (ALL CAPS)

To broaden your search results, use OR. The OR modifier requires that at least one of the terms you are searching for be present on the person's profile, in any order.

- Raytheon OR Boeing
- Pfizer OR Merck OR "Johnson and Johnson"

NOT (ALL CAPS)

When you want to exclude people from your search results, use NOT. You can also use a minus sign. This can be an extremely helpful modifier in removing irrelevant results.

- "Vice President" NOT "wealth management"
- Executive -Assistant

With just a little Boolean knowledge you can fine-tune your searches. We will be using Boolean throughout the remainder of this chapter, so it's important to familiarize yourself with it before moving forward.

Finding Business Owners

> Tom and his father specialized in working with business owners. With concerns about wealth transfer planning, succession planning, key-man insurance, and exit planning, they were ideal (and highly profitable) clients. Tom discovered that LinkedIn was a great place to find business owners and he became very proficient in doing so.

LinkedIn is fertile ground for B2B sales—you can't argue with the numbers. Hence, it has attracted many small-to-medium-sized business owners. Not only is their presence plentiful, but also determining mutual connections is easy (Fig. 22).

Step 1: Title Field

In the *Title* field, enter terms such as:

- Owner
- President
- CEO
- Franchise
- Principal
- Founder
- Co-Founder
- "Business Owner"
- "Sole Proprietor"
- "Self Employed"
- Self-Employed
- Entrepreneur
- Partner

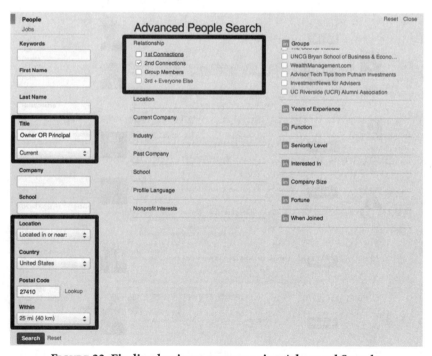

FIGURE 22: Finding business owners using Advanced Search.
Source: LinkedIn.

Notice we put phrases like "sole proprietor" in quotes because we are looking for an exact phrase. Also, once you put in your keyword, you can use the dropdown to identify *Current or past, Current, Past,* or *Past not current.* We would recommend you select *Current* if you want people who currently own businesses.

Step 2: Postal Code
Enter your postal code in the *Postal Code* field and select the desired distance from the *Within* dropdown box. (e.g., 25 miles from your location).

Step 3: Relationship
In the *Relationship* field, check the box for the type of connection you are targeting—*1st Connections, 2nd Connections, Group Members, 3rd + Everyone Else*—and run your search, sifting through the results for introduction opportunities. For most of the searches we conduct, we select *2nd Connections.* This means there is at least one person who can introduce us to the prospect.

If you have the premium version of LinkedIn, there is a filter for *Company Size.* Use this to zero in on your results and move beyond sole practitioners and individual consultants.

Run your search and review your search results for introduction opportunities. Make adjustments to your search parameters. If you have too many results, you may need to apply additional filters or reduce the location radius. If you don't have enough results, you may need to broaden your search results to loosen your parameters.

Running an Advanced Search for Someone who Sold Their Business
What if you are not interested in *current* business owners? Instead, you want to find people who sold a successful business (Fig. 23). You could repeat the previous search and only select *Past* under the *Title* field. This will give you plenty of results, but you don't really know if they went bankrupt or sold a business. Searching for these people takes

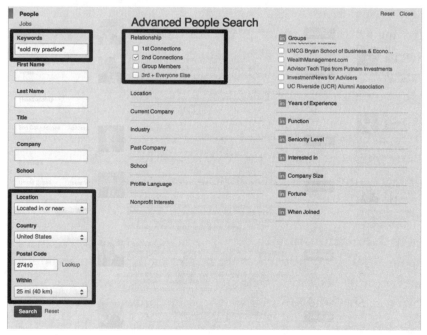

FIGURE 23: **Find people who sold their businesses. Source: LinkedIn.**

some patience and digging. A Google search can often help fill in the blanks.

Step 1: Keywords

Think about the types of phrases someone puts on their profile if they sold a business. Here are a few we like to use:

- "sold my business"
- "sold my practice"
- "sold my startup"
- "bought out"
- "recently sold"
- "grew my business"
- "we were acquired"

This is not a comprehensive list, but a great starting point. Take these phrases and put them in quotes in the *Keywords* field.

Step 2: Postal Code

Enter your postal code in the *Postal Code* field and select the desired distance from the *Within* dropdown box.

Step 3: Relationship

In the *Relationship* field, check the box for the type of connection you are targeting—*1st Connections, 2nd Connections, Group Members, 3rd + Everyone Else*—and run your search, sifting through the results for introduction opportunities. For our example, we selected *2nd Connections.*

Run your search and review your results. It's that simple.

Boolean Search String Examples

As you get better and better with Boolean, you will find it helpful to build and save search strings for your target market. You can store these in a simple notepad on your desktop. Then you can copy and paste Boolean search strings into the *Keywords, Title, Name,* and *Company* fields within LinkedIn's *Advanced Search* function.

Here is one we've built specifically for small-to-medium-sized business owners and people who've sold their business. In the search strings below, we included multiple synonyms of our targeted keywords and removed other financial professionals from the first search.

Business Owner Search String (Fig. 24)
(owner OR president OR CEO OR founder OR principal) -"financial advisor" -"investment manager" -"financial planning"

Sold a Business Search String
"sold my business" OR "sold my practice" OR "sold my startup" OR "recently sold" OR "grew my business" OR "bought out"

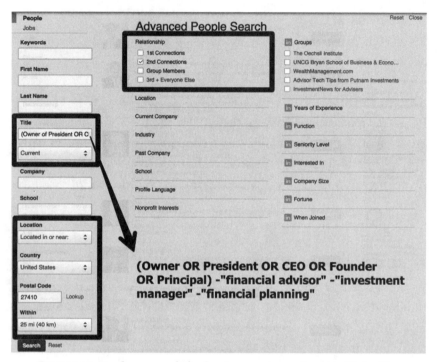

FIGURE 24: Boolean search for business owners. Source: LinkedIn.

Finding Money in Motion

Step back and consider the frame of mind of an average LinkedIn user. When many people first hear of LinkedIn, they think it's simply a place to network and find a job—an online resume. We know that LinkedIn is much more than that, but many people still use LinkedIn for this purpose alone. Perhaps they have been laid off or left their former employer. Often, this will trigger them to become more active on LinkedIn.

This means one thing for financial advisors—rollovers! Here is how LinkedIn's *Advanced Search* can help you find rollover opportunities (Fig. 25).

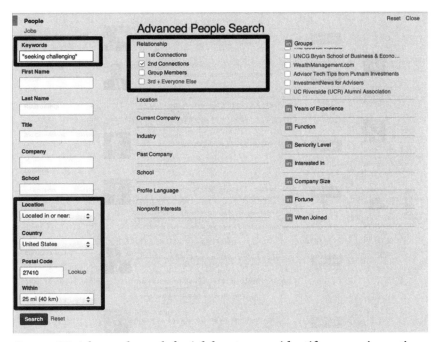

FIGURE 25: Advanced search for job hunters can identify money in motion.
Source: LinkedIn.

Step 1: Keywords

In the Keywords field enter terms such as:

- "new position"
- transition
- "seeking challenging"
- "career change"
- "great opportunity"
- "new opportunities"
- "actively seeking"
- "actively pursuing"
- "currently seeking"
- "new experience"
- "looking for"
- "at home"
- "in between jobs"
- "former executive"
- "former director"
- unemployed
- "laid off"
- available
- retired
- "recently retired"
- resigned
- "stepped down"
- "new career"

Also, if your search term is more than one word, make sure you put it in quotes. There are endless phrases and terms you can search for here. Just think about how people describe themselves on LinkedIn if they are between jobs. You will also notice we included the term "retired." You would be surprised by the number of retirees on LinkedIn.

Step 2: Postal Code
Enter your postal code in the *Postal Code* field and select the desired distance from the *Within* dropdown box.

Step 3: Relationship
In the *Relationship* field, check the box for the type of connection you are targeting—*1st Connections, 2nd Connections, Group Members, 3rd + Everyone Else*—and run your search. Review your results for prospects and introduction opportunities.

When asking for an introduction to someone who is between jobs, be upfront in your request. There's no reason to beat around the bush. Reach out to your 1st degree connection and mention the financial impact point you uncovered through LinkedIn. When doing so, you are explaining to the introducer (1st degree connection) why it makes sense for them to introduce you. You might say:

> *Jim, I noticed you are connected to Melissa Jones on LinkedIn and it looks like she is in between careers. I work with a lot of professionals in this position, and many times they need help rolling over their 401Ks from their former employers. How well do you know her? (WAIT FOR RESPONSE) I'd love your advice on the best way to reach out to her.*

If an introduction isn't possible, you may consider contacting this person directly. This is not ideal, but sometimes it's your only option. You'll find that most people who are using LinkedIn to find a job include their email and phone number on their profile. After all, they want potential employers to be able to reach them easily. Consider sending them an *InMail* or email, and as a last resort, you may even call them directly.

This search alone has resulted in numerous opportunities for the financial advisors we coach. With the amount of information available on social networks, the clues are out there. It's just a matter of finding them and making the *O-2-O Conversion*™ happen.

Boolean Search String Examples

The following is an example of a search string we've built to find money in motion. You will notice we've included multiple synonyms and phrases. Also, we have found that this search returns some Human Resource professionals who help people "in transition." We've eliminated some of these results by adding -*"Human Resources"* or -*recruiter* on the end of each search string. You can do the same thing if you notice financial service professionals by adding a -*"financial advisor"* or -*"investment manager"* or -*"financial planning."*

Money in Motion Search String (Fig. 26)
("currently seeking" OR "new opportunities" OR transition OR "new position" OR "seeking challenging" OR "career change" OR "seeking work" OR "new challenge" OR "seeking position") -recruiter -"head hunter" -"human resources"

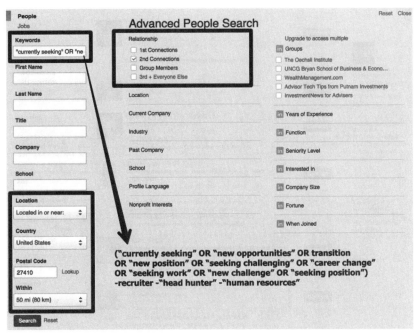

FIGURE 26: Money in motion Boolean search string. Source: LinkedIn.

Companies Downsizing

Another way to search for money in motion is to make a list of the companies in your local area that are downsizing. Then, simply run an advanced search for past employees of these companies. For example, if Hewlett-Packard is laying off a lot of employees in your area, your search may look like Figure 27 below:

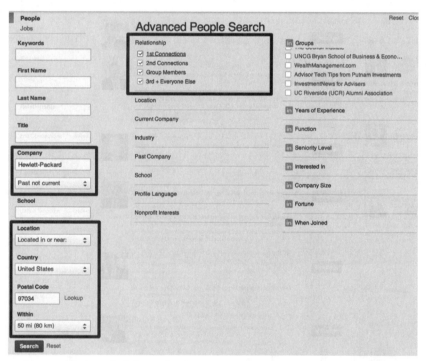

FIGURE 27: Search for employees leaving a company. Source: LinkedIn.

The key is making sure you denote *Past not current* under the *Company* field and input your postal code in the *Postal Code* field. Then, look through your results and determine the best course of action to contact each prospect.

WARN Act

A great way to gather a list of companies in your area that are laying people off is to take advantage of the Worker Adjustment and Retraining Notification Act. The WARN Act is a United States labor law which offers protection to workers, their families and communities by requiring employers to provide notice 60 days in advance of covered plant closings and covered mass layoffs.[16]

Run a Google search for the WARN Act in your state (Fig. 28). Review your results for a link to your state's website that contains the WARN Act. This may take a little digging.

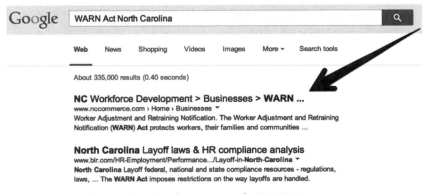

FIGURE 28: Google your state's WARN Act page.

Review your state's web page for the latest link to the WARN Act (Fig. 29). With just a couple clicks, you can find the WARN Act Notification report for your state with a list of companies that are downsizing.

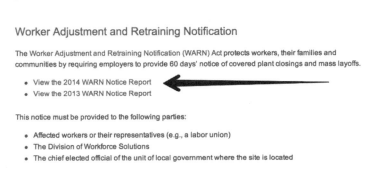

FIGURE 29: Locate the WARN Act notification report.

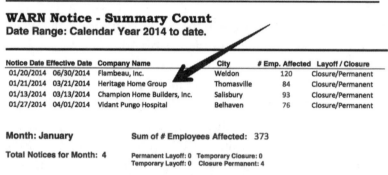

WARN Notice - Summary Count
Date Range: Calendar Year 2014 to date.

Notice Date	Effective Date	Company Name	City	# Emp. Affected	Layoff / Closure
01/20/2014	06/30/2014	Flambeau, Inc.	Weldon	120	Closure/Permanent
01/21/2014	03/21/2014	Heritage Home Group	Thomasville	84	Closure/Permanent
01/13/2014	03/13/2014	Champion Home Builders, Inc.	Salisbury	93	Closure/Permanent
01/27/2014	04/01/2014	Vidant Pungo Hospital	Belhaven	76	Closure/Permanent

Month: January   Sum of # Employees Affected: 373

Total Notices for Month: 4   Permanent Layoff: 0   Temporary Closure: 0
                          Temporary Layoff: 0   Closure Permanent: 4

FIGURE 30: WARN Act results.

Review the information in the WARN Act and look for companies you would like to target. The WARN Act will list the company name, effective date, as well as the number of employees affected. In Figure 30 is a section of the WARN Act results for North Carolina.

Take this information, and run an advanced search to find

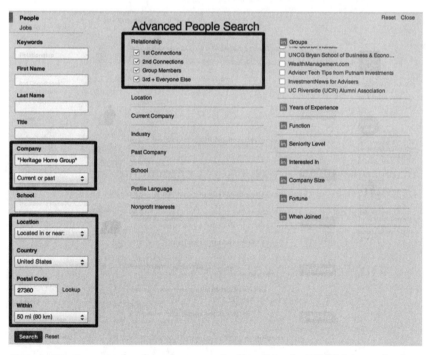

FIGURE 31: Once you've found companies listed in the WARN Act, take that info back to LinkedIn. Source: LinkedIn.

prospects being affected who work at those companies (Fig. 31). Make sure you put the correct company name in the *Company* field and enter an accurate postal code in the *Postal Code* field. You will also notice we broadened the relationship parameters for our search.

Use the same techniques as described in the previous section for reaching out to them. Ideally, leverage a 1st degree connection to meet them. Worst-case scenario, reach out to them directly.

Finding Centers of Influence (COIs)

After some time, Tom's father, who spent most of his time down in Florida, got the itch to get back into the prospecting game. He wanted to build relationships with CPAs and estate attorneys in Florida. The problem? He really didn't have much of a network in Florida (or so he thought).

His first attempt at building these relationships was purchasing a list and mass mailing letters to CPAs in his area. As he launched calls into these professionals, following up on his letter, he realized he was getting nowhere fast. He was also having nightmarish flashbacks to his days of cold calling on Wall Street as a rookie. His second attempt was to knock on doors. He showed up unannounced at a few offices in his area. While he got through a few gatekeepers, the reality set in that this would be a long process. Not to mention, he felt like he should be selling second-rate knives or vacuums.

Noting Tom's success using LinkedIn, he asked for his son's help. Tom was eager to show his father how he could find warm introduction opportunities to CPAs and attorneys by using LinkedIn.

Tom's first search found seven CPAs and three estate attorneys to which his father could get an introduction. You could have blown Tom's father over with a feather—he was amazed. Some of his 1st degree connections in their hometown of Philadelphia actually knew CPAs who lived in Naples! By leveraging LinkedIn as a search tool, Tom's father could keep his ego intact and engage in higher impact marketing activities.

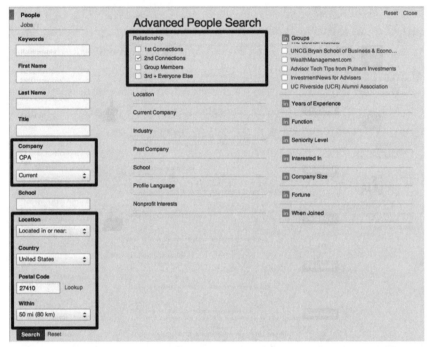

FIGURE 32: Example of an advanced search for CPAs. Source: LinkedIn.

There are endless ways to search for COIs on LinkedIn. Here is one we've found most effective (Fig. 32).

Step 1: Title

In the *Title* field, insert variations of the title that a CPA or estate attorney would list on a LinkedIn profile.

- CPA
- "Certified Public Accountant"
- Accountant
- "Senior Accountant"
- "Estate Attorney"
- Auditor
- "Estate Planning Attorney"
- "Estate Lawyer"

Also, make sure you select *Current* from the dropdown list under the *Title* field if you want COIs who are actively practicing.

Step 2: Postal Code

Enter your postal code in the *Postal Code* field and select the desired distance from the *Within* dropdown box. (e.g., 25 miles from your location).

Step 3: Relationship

In the *Relationship* field, check the box for the type of connection you are targeting—*1st Connections, 2nd Connections, Group Members, 3rd + Everyone Else*—and run your search. We recommend selecting *2nd Connections.* Run your search and review your results for introduction opportunities.

Boolean Search String Examples

The following are a few examples of search strings to help you find accountants and attorneys on LinkedIn. We used multiple synonyms for both professionals and removed most financial advisors from the accountant results (Fig. 33).

Accountant Search String
(CPA OR "Certified Public Accountant" OR "Tax Accountant" OR Accountant) -"financial plan" -"financial planning" -"financial advisor" -"investment management" -"wealth manager"

Estate Attorney Search String
"estate attorney" OR "estate plan" OR "trust and estate attorney" OR "estate planning" OR "estate lawyer"

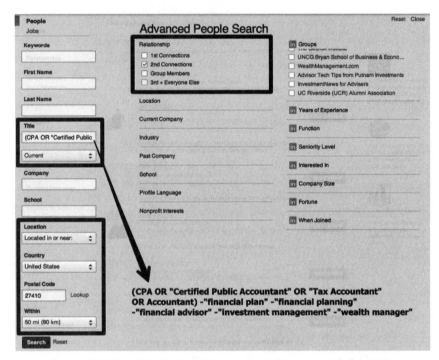

FIGURE 33: Use a Boolean string to strengthen a search for CPAs. Source: LinkedIn.

Finding Executives

According to a recent study, LinkedIn is the preferred social network for business executives.[17] If you target this market, LinkedIn is ripe with opportunity (Fig. 34).

Step 1: Title

Under the *Title* field, insert terms like:

- President
- Executive
- VP
- EVP
- V.P.
- Chief
- CIO
- CEO
- COO
- CFO
- CTO
- CMO
- "Vice President"

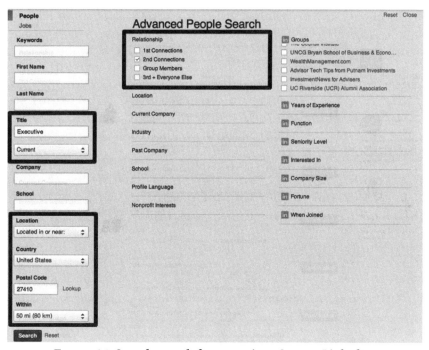

FIGURE 34: Sample search for executives. Source: LinkedIn.

If you are targeting executives from a particular company, the key is figuring out the hierarchy of positions and corresponding titles. Use those words in the *Title* field. Also, make sure you select *Current* from the dropdown list under the *Title* field if you want executives who currently hold their position.

Lastly, if you have the premium version of LinkedIn, you have an additional search filter available to you called *Seniority Level*. You may want to check the boxes for *CXO* and *VP* instead or in addition to using the terms above. You may also find the *Years of Experience* section helpful for fine-tuning your results.

Step 2: Company

Next, think of the companies your clients work for, or companies you want to infiltrate. Enter these names in the *Company* field on LinkedIn. Do some research to figure out how employees list the company name on their profiles. For example, do they put PwC or Pricewaterhouse Coopers?

You can also denote *Current or past* using the dropdown menu below the *Company* field.

Step 3: Postal Code

Enter your postal code in the *Postal Code* field and select the desired distance from the *Within* dropdown box. If the company you are targeting is not in close proximity to your current location, but you want to target them anyway, you may want to consider using the postal code for the company headquarters.

Step 4: Relationship

In the *Relationship* field, check the box for the type of connection you are targeting—*1st Connections, 2nd Connections, Group Members, 3rd + Everyone Else*—and run your search.

Boolean Search String Examples

Below are a few examples of search strings we've built to find corporate executives. We used multiple synonyms for our prospect's title. If you enter a specific company into the *Company* field you are targeting, you won't need to exclude financial advisors. However, if you do not input a company and are running a more general search for executives, you can minimize financial advisors showing up in the search results by using NOT (or the minus sign).

C-Suite Search String (Fig. 35)
(CEO OR COO OR CFO OR CMO OR CTO OR Executive OR EVP OR CIO) -"executive assistant" -"financial advisor" -"wealth manager" -"financial planner"

Vice President Search String
("Vice President" OR VP OR V.P.) -"financial advisor" -"wealth manager" -"financial plan" -"financial planner"

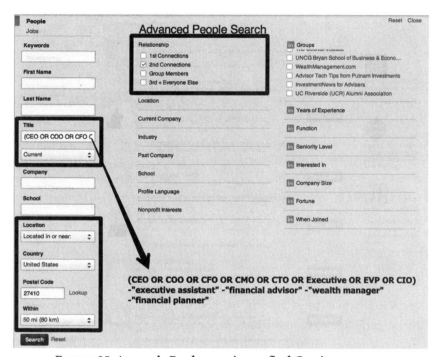

FIGURE 35: A sample Boolean string to find C-suite contacts.
Source: LinkedIn.

Adding Interests to Your Search

Whether you are searching for business owners, corporate executives, or people who changed jobs, if you can find prospects you share an affinity or interest with, you have a stronger likelihood of building rapport. Building rapport faster means building trust, which provides you with the necessary ingredients to be able to clinch the relationship and transform that connection into a client. It doesn't matter if your interests are skiing, golfing, opera, the Make-A-Wish Foundation, boating, or baking, someone out there has these interests on their profile—and you can search for it. Think of these as searches you can layer on top of those we just reviewed.

> Tom was an avid cyclist. He had cycled for years and found it an excellent way to prospect socially. By layering a search criterion for cycling he found he could connect with his prospects even faster. His initial approach would be to point out his mutual interest and start there. Once a conversation was taking place, he would arrange a face-to-face meeting, or even a ride. Once a relationship was established, he would then bring up business.
>
> Tom's father, down in Naples, was starting to meet with CPAs they had uncovered from their advanced searches. Tom's father found that layering on a search for *golf* was great for finding CPAs he could take out to his country club.

The easiest way to add an affinity to your search is under the *Keywords* section (Fig. 36). Under this section, add in the interest you are searching for and LinkedIn will scour profiles for those keywords. For cyclists, put in terms like *cycling* or *cyclist*. For golf, use *golfer, golf,* or *golfing.* Think about the different iterations of the interests or hobbies someone might put on a profile.

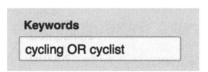

FIGURE 36: Using keywords.
Source: LinkedIn.

Remember, you will want to include your other search criterion, but you are adding an interest layer in the *Keywords* field. Once you find prospects with interests similar to your own, mention the interest when you ask for an introduction or reach out directly.

Special Interest Searches for Your Events

Want more prospects at your intimate events? If you have an intimate event on the horizon, such as a golf clinic, wine tasting, or fishing excursion, use the special interest search to find prospects your 1st degree connections can bring along to your event. You can do this two ways:

1. **Using the *Advanced Search***

   Click on the *Advanced Search* link and under the *Keywords* field input the affinity you are targeting, in this case *golf.* Make sure you select *2nd Connections* under the *Relationship* field and also input your postal code in the *Postal Code* field (Fig. 37).

   Review your results for 2nd degree connections that your 1st degree connections could bring along to your intimate event.

2. **Searching your connection's connections**

   Go to the profile page of someone you plan to invite to your upcoming golf clinic event. Scroll down on their page to see a preview of their connections. In the upper right hand corner, click

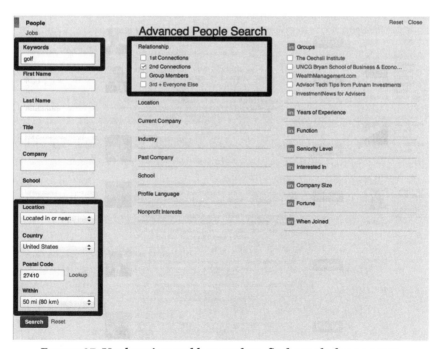

FIGURE 37: Use location and keywords to find people for an event.
Source: LinkedIn.

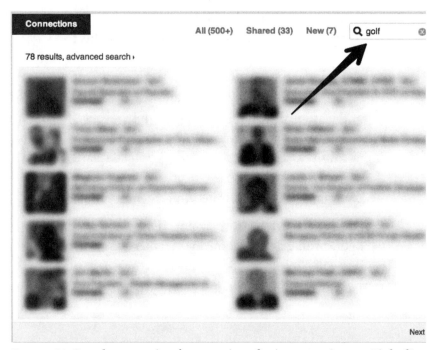

Connections

All (500+)   Shared (33)   New (7)   Q golf

78 results, advanced search ›

Next

FIGURE 38: Search connections' connections for interests. Source: LinkedIn.

on the magnifying glass and a search box will appear (Fig. 38). Enter your desired interest into the search box, in this case *golf.*

Run your search and you will get a list of your 1st degree connection's connections who have *golf* listed on their profile. You've just built a great invite list to your event.

Here's some language you can use when calling up your client (1st degree connection) to ask them to bring someone to your client event.

Mr. Client, I'm excited you will be joining us for our golf clinic next Friday. It's going to be a great event. I lined up one of the best pros at the course.

As you recall, everyone is bringing someone and I noticed you are connected to William Mitchell on LinkedIn. He lists that he plays golf on his LinkedIn profile. Do you think he would want to come? He looks like the type of person I'd like to meet anyway.

Remember, have another name or two in your back pocket in case the 1st degree connection doesn't know the first prospect you mentioned well enough to invite them.

Saving Searches

Running advanced searches is an excellent way to source new prospects and COIs. But running these searches can be a very manual and time-intensive process. Can you imagine going in every week and running this search?

(CEO OR COO OR CFO OR CMO OR CTO OR Executive OR EVP OR CIO) -"executive assistant" -"financial advisor" -"wealth manager" -"financial planner"

No thanks! It's also easy to forget to run the search on a regular basis, but it's important to do so because your network is constantly evolving, and your search results are ever-changing. This is why using the *Save Search* feature is important.

With the free version of LinkedIn, you can save up to three searches. Take advantage of this great perk. This will allow you to get a list of potential prospects delivered to your email inbox each week without having to lift a finger. Once you have saved a search, you can program LinkedIn to send you a weekly or monthly alert. This alert includes *new* people who match the criteria you specified in your search.

Once you run an advanced search you like, select the *Save Search* link in the upper right hand corner of your screen (Fig. 39).

You will then have an option to title your search and set the notification frequency. Be specific when titling your search so you can easily

FIGURE 39: Don't be a sucker. Save that search. Source: LinkedIn.

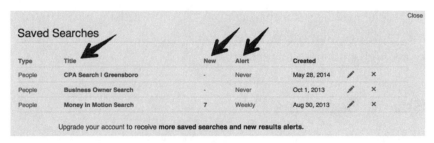

FIGURE 40: Alerts on searches do the work for you. Source: LinkedIn.

recall it later. LinkedIn will then send you an email with new results (Fig. 40). You can also check back and review your saved searches periodically to see a list of the new results. In the saved searches above, you will notice we have seven new results from our *Money in Motion Search*. It looks like we have some prospects to reach out to!

Filtering by Age Group

How helpful would it be to run a search by age? By making a few assumptions on graduation date, you can generate a reasonably targeted list in a few simple steps by leveraging LinkedIn's *Find Alumni* feature. This is the only way to search by age on LinkedIn.

Step 1: Access the *Find Alumni* Feature

From your profile page, select *Connections* in the top menu, and then select *Find Alumni* (Fig. 41).

Step 2: Select Your Targeted University

When the feature opens, it will default to the most recent school you attended, but you can select any university using the *Change School* dropdown toward the upper right side of your window. Your university and local universities are an ideal place to start.

Step 3: Filter for Age Group

Suppose you are looking for 65-year-olds. Assuming a common college graduation age of 22, simply count back 43 years (65 - 22 = 43) to find

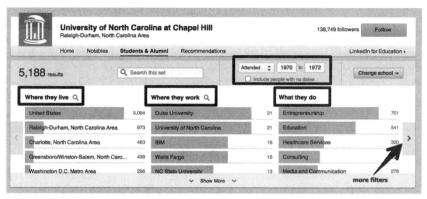

FIGURE 41: **Find Alumni helps you roughly filter by age and other useful categories. Source: LinkedIn.**

the year most 65-year-olds graduated. In this case, the year would be 1971, so you might enter the range of 1970 to 1972 in the search. LinkedIn will return results of alumni who attended during that time frame, not just those who graduated in one of those years.

Step 4: Apply Additional Filters

There are six bar charts that let you further parse out contacts according to parameters in the following categories: *Where they live, Where they work, What they do, What they studied, What they're skilled at,* and *How you are connected.* Simply click on the bar or bars you wish to include in your search.

Step 5: Use Keyword Searches

Above the bar charts is a magnifying glass that you can use to further refine your search by entering keywords (Fig. 42). For instance, if you have a niche of serving dentists, you might type *dentist* in the magnifying glass under *What they're skilled* at to find a list of dentists in your target age range.

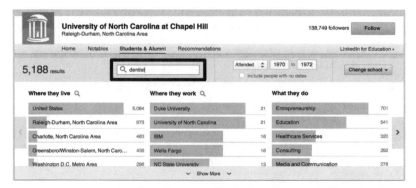

FIGURE 42: **Go further than standard Alumni Search filters with keyword search. Source: LinkedIn.**

Advanced Search: Your LinkedIn Routine

The Advanced Search feature on LinkedIn is one of the most powerful, but it doesn't have to take up the most time. Here are some actions to consider adding to your LinkedIn routine.

ACTION STEPS TO CONSIDER:

- Review your saved search results when you receive them via email. You should have saved results for things like money in motion, business owners, COIs, executives, or whatever other niche you target.
- Run an advanced search a few times a week for searches you don't have saved. Add and remove filters to vary your results; there are always ways to fine-tune your searches. Review the results and look for prospects.

CHAPTER 7

Groups

Why join the navy if you can be a pirate?

—Steve Jobs, cofounder of Apple

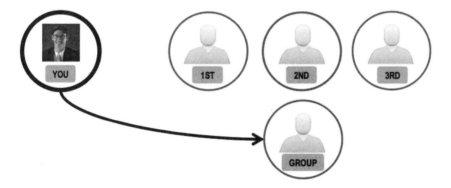

You've probably already joined a handful of LinkedIn groups. When you created your account, you were eager to join these niche communities of people who shared similar interests. But you quickly became frustrated with spammers who invaded poorly managed groups. The content wasn't helpful or relevant. You probably got useless group digest emails, and the perceived value of LinkedIn groups diminished. You lost interest.

We would urge you to reconsider. Don't let these poorly managed groups leave a bad taste in your mouth. There are currently millions of groups on LinkedIn and your future prospects are in them. It's really just a matter of finding the right groups and building real-world relationships. They are a niche marketer's dream come true.

Finding Groups to Join

Find Basic Groups

LinkedIn lets you join up to 50 groups with the free version, but the truth is, you don't have time to actively participate in 50 groups. So focus on 10 to 15 to which you can actually devote your time.

Start by joining some basic groups in which you have a genuine interest. Here are some examples of basic groups we recommend you join:

- Alumni groups (e.g., UCLA Alumni)
- Professional peer groups (e.g., Financial Advisor Network)
- Professional development groups (e.g., Oechsli Institute)
- Industry news groups (e.g., WealthManagement.com)
- Professional designation groups (e.g., Certified Financial Planner)
- Charitable groups (e.g., Make-A-Wish)

Find Targeted Groups

Outside of groups being great places to learn amongst your peers and other industry experts, they are excellent places to cultivate new prospects. Refer back to your *Ideal Prospect Profile.* If you recall, we answered questions about the prospects you are targeting, such as:

- What company do (did) they work for?
- What industry are they a part of?
- What is their job title?
- Where do they live?
- What are their hobbies?
- What charities and organizations are they involved in?

We guarantee there is a group that satisfies nearly every answer to the questions from your *Ideal Prospect Profile.* Take your *Ideal Prospect Profile* and search the group's directory. In the main search form at the top of the page, select *groups* from the dropdown menu to the left of the search box.

Next, enter terms that describe the type of group you are looking for. If you work with a highly targeted niche, look for similar groups on LinkedIn. Also, adding a location keyword will help you find groups in your area. Ultimately, this will help the *O-2-O Conversion™*. Keep in mind that you can combine your answers together with some simple Boolean modifiers to really target your search (Fig. 43). (e.g., *Raytheon AND Raleigh or "Business Owners" AND "St. Louis"*)

FIGURE 43: **Sample group search using
a Boolean modifier. Source: LinkedIn.**

Below are additional examples of searches to find targeted groups (Fig. 44). The key is trying multiple variations until you find what you are looking for. This process takes a little trial and error. Here are a number of examples and the search results they return.

If you are targeting startup companies in Boston, you might try:
startup AND Boston

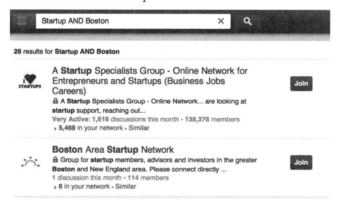

If you work primarily with engineers in Portland you might try:
Engineers AND Portland

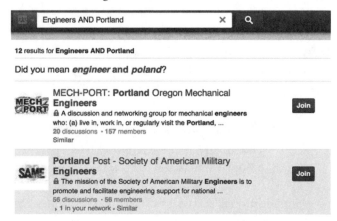

If you work with successful Indians in Silicon Valley you might try:
Indians AND "San Francisco"

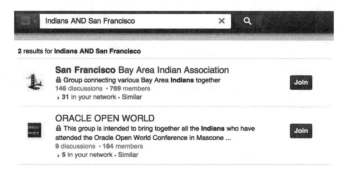

If you target successful Jewish professionals in Chicago you might try:
Jewish AND Chicago

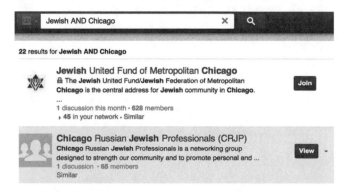

If you are targeting attorneys who went to the University of Michigan you might try: *"University of Michigan" AND Law*

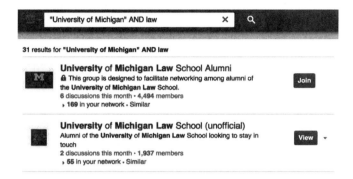

If you are targeting retirees from Pfizer: *Pfizer AND retirees*

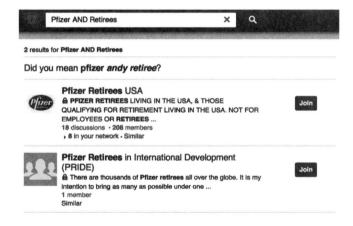

FIGURE 44: Six examples above of Boolean search combinations and their results. Source: LinkedIn.

There are endless groups and combinations of searches you can try. Many of the groups you are targeting may be locked, meaning that getting into the group requires approval by the group manager. The truth is, most group managers are not very strict about who they let in the group, so it's always worth a try. If you are still denied entry, identify the group owner or manager and message them directly on LinkedIn. Tell them why it makes sense for you to be a part of the group and let them know your intentions. It never hurts to ask.

Posting, Listening, and Searching in Groups

Now you've found some great groups and requested to join. The next step is to build relationships and make the *O-2-O Conversion*™ happen.

Posting in Groups

Once you are accepted into these groups, you will be tempted to start promoting your professional services. Resist this temptation! Your first step is to position yourself as a valuable member. You can accomplish this by commenting and liking others' posts, posting helpful information, and posing questions. Just remember, keep it relevant to the group. Once you are viewed as a valuable and trusted contributor, you can sprinkle in a few promotional posts (e.g., an invitation to your educational event on social security).

When you make a post and someone engages with you, great! That's an invitation to start a conversation. In the example below (Fig. 45), a financial advisor posted a helpful article and a prospect commented on his post. Now, he could message the prospect directly or request a connection.

Listening in Groups

Don't underestimate the power of listening within your LinkedIn groups. Look for posts where you can step in and demonstrate your ex-

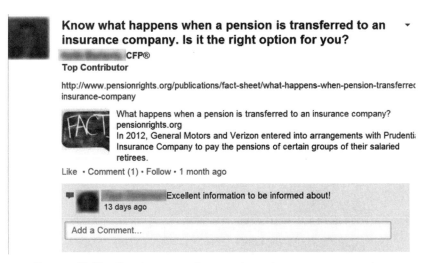

FIGURE 45: Posting to groups is a great way to engage prospects.
Source: LinkedIn.

pertise. Once you see this type of post, you can message or ask the prospect to connect.

Some signals are more obvious than others. In the example below (Fig. 46), we spotted a post within a group of a person asking a question about his upcoming job interview. If he isn't in transition already, he will be soon! This means there may be a rollover opportunity. These types of clues can be found throughout various LinkedIn groups and are excellent opportunities to cultivate relationships with prospects.

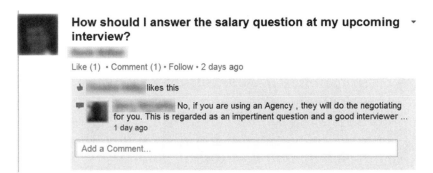

FIGURE 46: Sit back and watch, as prospects drop clues in LinkedIn groups.
Source: LinkedIn.

Searching the Member Directory

We know what you're thinking. You wouldn't expect to do business with a lot of the people in these groups. In fact, there are probably people just like you within these groups. It's true. But one of the best features of LinkedIn groups is getting access to the member directory. Within this member directory, you can search for your ideal prospects.

Start by clicking on the *members* link in the upper right hand corner of the group's page (Fig. 47). In the example below, you would have access to 9,126 members!

FIGURE 47: **Access group members to sift through the gold mine.**
Source: LinkedIn.

Next, run a keyword search within the member directory (Fig. 48). Think about the types of keywords your ideal prospect would have on their profile, and run a search. In the example below, we are looking for business owners. We also used the Boolean modifier OR to broaden our search.

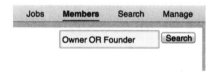

FIGURE 48: **Member keyword search. Source: LinkedIn.**

Once you engage the search, you will then have options to *Send message* or *Connect* (Fig. 49). Let's explore both options.

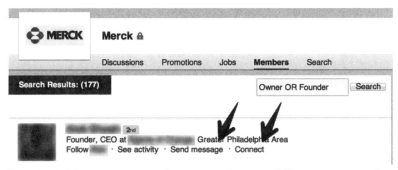

FIGURE 49: There are two options to reach out to fellow group members.
Source: LinkedIn.

Connecting and Messaging Group Members

Connecting with Group Members

Now that you have presented yourself as a valuable member and searched the member directory to find prospects, it's time to make contact. If possible, we recommend you ask for an introduction. However, if this is not possible, you will need to send a message or request to connect. Let's review the most effective way to draft a connection request for a fellow group member.

The first thing you should mention in your connection request is the group in which you are both members. This will make them much more receptive to your message. Something as simple as:

Hi Jim, we are both members of the University of Michigan Alumni Group . . .

Second, you need to personalize the message. You can do this by referencing a post they contributed, a person you both know, something you read about their company, something you noticed on their LinkedIn profile, or any other reference point you notice. Now you've planted the seeds for a personal relationship.

I graduated in 1990. Go Blue! I really enjoyed your post on work-life balance the other day. Great tips! I would love to connect.

Your call to action when requesting to connect is just that—to connect. Don't try to ask for a business meeting or social get-together yet; it's too early. It's important that you make a genuine effort to build real relationships with group members and not just pitch a sale. This strategy is about nurturing relationships.

Welcome to modern-day networking. LinkedIn groups create an excellent forum to prospect at scale and broaden your network like never before.

Messaging Group Members

What if you don't want to connect? Instead, you just want to send a message. Perhaps you want to send hundreds of messages and take a colder prospecting approach. Here's the great thing, and a lesser-known fact, about LinkedIn groups:

Groups give you the ability to message other group members even if they are outside of your network.

If you want to send a message to someone who is a 2nd degree or 3rd degree connection with no common groups, LinkedIn wants you to pay for *InMails* (upgrade to a Premium account). Most people have the free version of LinkedIn, and while there may be certain scenarios where sending *InMails* makes sense, you can save your *InMails* by leveraging the communication capabilities of groups.

Just like in your request to connect, the first step in messaging group members is to reference the group you share.

Hi Jim, we are both members of the Merck Group . . .

Next, you need to get to the point of your message—fast. If your objective is to ask for a business meeting, explain to the prospect why it would be beneficial for them. If your objective is to invite them to your upcoming webinar, you might say:

We've worked with a number of Merck executives over the years and helped them manage their financial affairs. We are holding a webinar next Tuesday at 12pm ET answering the top five questions we

get from Merck executives like you regarding their retirement. We
would love for you to join us.

If you're interested, here is the link to register (http://www.xyz.com)
If I can answer any additional questions about the webinar, don't hes-
itate to reach out. I hope you can join us.
—Matt

You could literally send this message to hundreds of fellow group
members.

Important! If you do not see an option to send a message, the user
has blocked this functionality. This might be a time when it's appropriate to send an *InMail* or invite someone to connect with a personalized
message. That said, most users let group members message them, so
use this tactic to send as many messages to your target market at no
charge.

Creating Your Own Group

Ron had been an advisor in his community for nearly 20 years and had
a great reputation. The problem was, his business wasn't growing. But
Ron was also an out-of-the-box thinker, and he was convinced that
LinkedIn would be the next big thing to help grow his business. He just
wasn't sure how he should approach it.

When his wife received a package in the mail from a Fortune 100
company regarding the termination of her pension, it hit him. There
would be millions upon millions of dollars in motion in the next few
months. Current and past employees had to determine what to do with
the money in their soon-to-be-terminated pensions. Do they take a
lump sum or annuity? Roll it over into an IRA? There were a lot of unan-
swered questions.

Ron decided to create his own LinkedIn group to address the issue.
He positioned the group as a resource for current and past employees
whose pensions were being terminated. He posted helpful articles, resources, and answered questions.

Within one month of creating his group, and without any promotion, Ron had 485 members, essentially prospects. They were posing

questions and looking for answers. A few people discovered the group organically and joined. When they joined, their connections (colleagues) took notice and they decided to join. Before he knew it, Ron's group had practically gone viral.

The icing on the cake was that Ron was in complete control of who could enter the group, so he made sure to screen out any competitors. Prospects were posting questions and Ron's new problem was not *finding prospects*, it was how to deal with all the prospects *finding him*.

Creating your own group can be a viable strategy for attracting your target market to you, creating a magnetic effect. Creating groups is easy, only takes a few minutes to get started, and is a great way to quickly expand your network. But it does require a bit of work and diligence to be successful.

The idea is for you to connect with your target market based on a mutual interest, passion, need, or area of commonality. You want to create a group that is a resource to your market and then ultimately leverage it for business purposes. This takes time and a strategy.

Examples of Types of Groups to Create

There are endless types of groups you could create. Below are a few ideas we've seen work well.

- **Networking Group:** Create a group that's specific to your location and designed for other professionals to network. This is a great way to network with current and potential COIs. One advisor we coached created a general networking group for his small town that now has more than 5,000 members!

- **Resource for Employees:** If there are particular companies in your area downsizing (see WARN Act) or that you target in general, create a group full of helpful resources for the employees in transition. Another financial advisor we worked with created a group for Air Force officers in transition.

- **Affinity Groups:** If you have a passion or hobby that attracts your ideal prospect, create a group around it. For example, one advisor we coached created a local cycling group where he planned rides so he could meet face to face with members.

Name Your Group

The actual name you select for your group is important. When considering names for your group, put yourself in your ideal prospect's shoes. Try to determine what keywords or phrases your prospects would search and name your group accordingly. Also, include similar keywords in the description of the group. If you wanted to create a local wine group, you would want to use the word *wine* in the name and maybe a local reference such as *San Francisco Wine Lovers.*

Create a Logo

Adding a logo to your group will make it more appealing and some members will even display your logo on their profile. You want your logo to look professional and clean. If it's a wine group, use a wine bottle as a logo. If it's a networking group, use a photo of hands shaking and perhaps the name of your city. It should be simple and easy to understand.

Get Exposure

Including your group in the *Group Directory* and allowing members to post the group logo on their profile, will help gain you more exposure naturally. These settings can be managed in the *Group Settings.*

Keep it Local?

Consider your ultimate goal. If you are selling a product or service that will ultimately require you to build rapport through face-to-face contact, which we suspect the majority of readers are, then you may want to keep your group local. This should be clearly labeled in your group's summary and description.

Growing and Managing Your Group

A group with no members is of little value. Once your group is live, it's time to start inviting people. Begin by inviting people that are interested in the content associated with your group. You can start with your 1st degree connections. When logged into the group, select the *share group* feature (Fig. 50).

FIGURE 50: This button allows you to share your group.
Source: LinkedIn.

You can then share an update, post to groups, or send to individuals. Start by sending a message to individuals (Fig. 51). Type in the names of your 1st degree connections that you would like to invite and personalize a message to them.

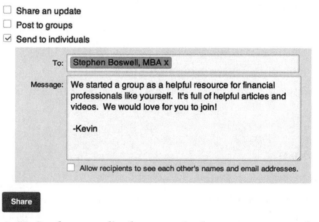

FIGURE 51: Send personalized notes to invite new group members.
Source: LinkedIn.

You can also ask members to help you grow your group. Send a message to members or post a topic that is designed to encourage people to invite others to join. Sometimes setting a specific goal for group membership can encourage everyone to spread the word. For example, let your members know that your goal is to reach 1,000 members, and that you need their help to do it.

Also, when posting to other groups, do your best to link the message back to your group when it's appropriate. Let people know you created a group to address whatever question they are posting. You want your group to gain as much exposure as possible.

Managing Content and Engagement

It's important that you post content and links that are of interest to your group on a regular basis. Your objective is to create interaction between yourself and members by being a resource. This starts by posting useful content frequently. You can also ask other non-competing experts to become members and post information.

You will also need to manage your group. Similar to tending a garden, if your group isn't managed regularly it can get out of hand! Check for anyone in the group who is posting promotional materials or information not pertinent to the group. Don't let your group turn "spammy." This will turn other members off. Also, continue to weed out competitors, as like *kudzu*, they will continue to come back.

> In Ron's case, he made sure to load up his group with plenty of helpful articles before he invited anyone. He wanted to make sure that people's first impressions of the group were good ones. As people posed questions, he would find other resources to help guide them. Other members began answering each other's questions as well.

Converting Your Group Members into Clients

> After a month, Ron's group was alive. The group was growing consistently and the engagement was fantastic. While Ron's LinkedIn group was growing, his business still wasn't. With some coaching on our end, we put together a strategy for him to develop these online relationships into real-world business opportunities. The secret to Ron's success was slowly and steadily progressing each individual relationship with group members. It was done one relationship at a time, over time.

With the right strategy, you can increase engagement and convert group members into clients. Think of converting group members as a progression that builds over time from personal contact. Here are some of our favorite tactics.

Personal Welcome Message

The moment a new person joins your group, reach out to them individually. Send a personalized message to connect. The goal of the message is to add this person to your network, but you also want to do the following:

- Raise awareness about you being the owner of the group
- Reinforce the purpose of the group
- Ask the newest member if there are specific questions they would like answered from the group
- Ask the new members to post within the group to introduce themselves and stimulate interaction. This is more appropriate for networking and small affinity groups.

You might say:

Thanks so much for joining our group. I moderate this group and wanted to introduce myself. The purpose is to be a resource for XYZ employees as they work through the recent pension terminations and the options available.

If you have any particular questions you would like answered, please don't hesitate to post them.

I would love to add you to my network.

—Matt

Offer Networking Support

After a week or so, send the newest members of your group a personal message to position yourself as a *Giver*. This can be as simple as a quick message offering networking support. Send a personalized message and include a line in your message such as:

*If I can ever be of assistance from a networking perspective, let me
know.*

We understand that this may take a bit of time, which we recognize
is at a premium. For advisors, this can be a perfect assignment for an
intern. They're typically current in the latest technology and social
media trends and can easily send a message on your behalf.

Send Helpful Content

Periodically send prospects you've connected with personalized messages on LinkedIn. These need to be helpful! Send them pertinent articles, videos and more.

Take Group Interaction Offline

As group members begin posting and engaging, look for opportunities
to answer their questions offline. Figure 52 shows a real-life example of
a prospect proposing a question within an advisor's LinkedIn group.

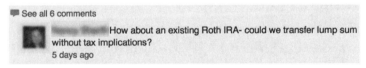

**FIGURE 52: A question presents a prime opportunity to connect.
Source: LinkedIn.**

This is how you might respond and convert this prospect:

1. Answer the prospect's question generically and promptly. You
   should also mention that you'll contact her privately with more
   information. This is so other group members know what is happening behind the scenes and it doesn't look like you are ignoring the prospect.
2. If you haven't already, you should ask the prospect to connect
   personally.
3. Lastly, make the *O-2-O Conversion*™ happen by requesting a
   face-to-face meeting or telephone conversation to address her
   question in more detail.

Exclusive Event for Members

If your group is local, you can plan a local meeting with members of your group. This allows for interaction and the necessary rapport-building before venturing down the path of a business discussion. Remember, this is the ultimate goal. You want to expand your network and turn online prospects into viable face-to-face opportunities. Figure 53 is an excellent real-life example.

FIGURE 53: Image of a great, real-life group event invite. Source: LinkedIn.

Requesting a Conversation

For prospects in your group who are not asking questions, once a solid online rapport has been established, and you've truly positioned yourself as a *Giver*, it's time to make the *O-2-O Conversion*™ happen. Send them a message and invite them to have a quick phone conversation, coffee, or lunch. The objective is to get to know them—build rapport and trust. During your first meeting, learn about them and how you can help. Of course, there will be a time for you to explain what you do, but don't make this conversation about you. Your goal is to build a real-world relationship.

> *Hi Matt,*
>
> *Thanks for connecting recently. I hope you've found the group and some of the articles I've been sending helpful. I also noticed we have a number of connections in common—small world.*
>
> *I've been working with numerous employees of XYZ helping them make decisions based on the pension termination.*

Everyone's situation is unique. Are you open to a 15-minute call to discuss your specific situation?

—Kevin

Ron found the most value in his local events. He would secure space at a restaurant and give a brief presentation on the pension termination scenarios. Afterwards, he mingled with attendees and got to know them personally. This improved the comfort level of attendees and they started to trust him. Ron's LinkedIn group has been an excellent source of new business.

Groups: Your LinkedIn Routine

You shouldn't try to be actively involved in 50 groups. While it may be tempting, it's really not feasible. By now, you should be involved in 10 to 15 groups, monitoring their interactions daily (or weekly at a minimum).

ACTION STEPS TO CONSIDER:

- Review your groups that contain prospects and look for recent posts. If a prospect posts something interesting, make sure you comment or like their post. If appropriate, ask them to connect. If a prospect poses a question to the group that you can answer—make the *O-2-O Conversion*™ happen! Send a message and offer to help via phone or Skype.
- Once a week, run a search in the member directory to find a potential prospect to reach out to. Remember, you can save your *InMails* by doing it this way. Send a direct message through the group for free.
- Contribute to the group! Look for helpful articles that are pertinent to your groups. If you have content you've developed, use it! Also, comment and add value to other people's posts. Really contribute.

- If you have your own group, management is key. Log in daily and remove promotional posts and spam. Managing and monitoring your group can be a perfect assignment for an intern.
- If you have your own group, direct message and connect with all new members who have business potential. Introduce yourself as the group owner.
- If you have your own group, continue to provide value by being a *Giver*. Build up enough equity with members to make the *O-2-O Conversion*™ happen.

CHAPTER **8**

COIs (Centers of Influence)

All you need to grow fine, vigorous grass is a crack in your sidewalk.

—Will Rogers, humorist and social commentator

Bob is a 25-year veteran who fell in love with LinkedIn. Unlike many advisors his age (Bob's in his 50s), he didn't delegate LinkedIn to his junior; to the contrary, he called our office and engaged a coach. He wanted to learn how to fish for himself.

His enthusiasm and creativity led to us creating a LinkedIn presentation that was designed to educate CPAs and estate attorneys on how to use LinkedIn to grow their businesses. Bob knew that these professionals didn't know a fraction of what he had learned on how to use LinkedIn. He sent out an email and LinkedIn invites to his targeted list of COIs and the response was overwhelming. He conducted a 90-minute workshop with nearly 50 COIs in attendance!

On the surface it appeared that Bob had hit a homerun. But that wasn't the case. The group was so large he wasn't able to make personal connections. Bob soon learned that less is more.

Cultivating COI relationships can provide incredible leverage and scale for accomplishing your business growth objectives. Our research points out that building relationships with COIs is one of the top strategies used by *Elite Advisors* (Table 6). It's worth incorporating a COI strategy into your marketing campaign, as the right relationships can be excellent sources of new business.

Table 6: Elite Advisors' Very Frequently Used Marketing Activities[2]

Introductions	46%
Referral Alliances	46%
Networking	43%
Directly Generated Referrals	21%
Client Events	18%
Indirectly Generated Referrals	14%
Seminars	4%
Direct Mail	0%
Cold Calling	0%

Source: Oechsli Institute

LinkedIn is just one arrow in your quiver when it comes to building these professional relationships, but it can be a powerful one. This chapter should provide you with some fresh ways to add value to these professional relationships using LinkedIn.

Teach Your COIs How to Use LinkedIn

Bob's large-scale LinkedIn presentations to COIs seemed great on the surface, but didn't produce the results he wanted—referrals. He decided to take a more intimate approach. Instead of a large-scale presentation, he would invite individual COIs to his office over lunch. During this meeting, he would share his LinkedIn knowledge and show them how they could grow their own businesses with LinkedIn. He found that during these intimate meetings the conversation blossomed from LinkedIn, to how that COI was growing their business, to the types of clients the COI served best. The conversation would also take a personal tone and Bob could actually build rapport. Bob was able to establish personal relationships with COIs in this manner, and these relationships became the foundation of his marketing success.

Remember, part of your LinkedIn strategy is to be a *Giver*, this includes sharing your knowledge about LinkedIn. Even if you're a novice LinkedIn user, you're probably further ahead of more people than you think. It is not uncommon for users to create an account without thinking through a strategy on how it could be used.

Draw on what you know so far, including the information in this book (maybe even gift a copy of this book—shameless plug), to start a conversation with CPAs, attorneys and other COIs about improving their LinkedIn strategies. Doing so could not only endear you to the COI, but also open them up to the world of social selling. And as their instructor, you will reap the benefits. It's a strategy that can help everyone involved.

Step 1: Invite

Invite your COIs to join you, one-on-one, for a "LinkedIn lunch" to share ideas. During this pre-meeting call, inquire about your COI's LinkedIn usage to help you create an agenda for the meeting. You might ask:

- *How do you currently use LinkedIn?*
- *How do you use it for business purposes?*
- *Do you use LinkedIn for prospecting?*
- *Are your clients on LinkedIn?*
- *Do your prospects look you up online?*

Step 2: Meet

Meet for lunch, but be certain to leave your sales cap at home. The meeting is not about how *you* might benefit from your COI using LinkedIn. Instead, it's about opening up a dialogue and sharing ideas around LinkedIn. Dialogue about:

- Branding: first impressions of each other's profiles (keep the tone friendly, but constructive)
- Gathering intelligence: connecting with clients and following their companies
- Prospecting: using LinkedIn's *Advanced Search* to find prospects.

For CPAs, you might show them how to search for CFOs or tax directors. You can also have them complete the *Ideal Prospect Profile* exercise in Chapter 3.

Step 3: Follow Up

From this point forward, your objective is to become your COI's LinkedIn confidant and keep the dialogue and idea-sharing alive. Send your COIs helpful articles on LinkedIn tips and offer introductions to your contacts. Once you've earned their trust, you can ask for introductions as well.

Many COIs are late to the LinkedIn party. Showing them a new tool that will help them grow their business puts you in a position to reap the rewards again and again.

LinkedIn List Sharing with COIs

Bob was eager to build relationships with COIs, but uneasy about one major (and important) aspect. As he put it, "It's always been a one-way street with my referral alliance partners. I send referrals and that's it. There is no reciprocation. Sometimes I feel like maybe I'm wasting my time."

With a little prodding on our part, we were able to not only help Bob provide valuable referrals to his COIs, we also tripled the number of referrals he was receiving. Here's the process we coached him through.

This next strategy is all about being a *Giver.* It's about providing copious amounts of value first, and letting the law of reciprocity kick in.

Step 1: Contact Your COI

Call up a COI with whom you have a good relationship, and ask them to catch up over lunch or coffee. After they agree and you set a date, explain that you are going to bring a list of your LinkedIn connections to go through with them. You might say the following:

Mrs. CPA, I wanted to catch up over lunch when you have a second. When can we put something on the calendar? (WAIT FOR RE-SPONSE) By the way, I'm going to bring a list of some of my LinkedIn connections. Let's see if there is anyone you might want to meet.

Step 2: Do Your Homework

Before your meeting, do your homework. You don't want to peruse hundreds of connections while meeting your COI. Instead, go through your connection base ahead of time and identify people your COI may have an interest in meeting. Develop a short list of 10 to 15 potential introductions for them.

Step 3: Share Your List

Keep your meeting with the COI casual and light. But at some point during your meeting, pull out your list and let them know you've found a few people they might find of interest. You might say the following:

Mrs. COI, I found a handful of my 1st degree connections on LinkedIn who might be good potential clients for you. Can we go through them? If you find any who look interesting, I would be happy to introduce you.

Because you are adding so much value, you will find that most COIs will offer to reciprocate. While you should not approach this meeting solely for reciprocity, it's a great and very common result.

Bob held these types of meetings with a handful of COIs. Every single COI thanked him profusely and offered to reciprocate. As one of the COIs thanked Bob, she mentioned, "This was great. Next time let's do my connections." Bob's pipeline and relationships with these COIs have never been better.

COIs: Beyond CPAs and Attorneys

There are millions of professionals on LinkedIn. So there is no need to limit yourself to the traditional CPA and attorney partners when you have access to other professionals who come in contact with those who fit your *Ideal Prospect Profile*. Below is a list of other professionals you might consider.

- High-end realtors
- Private equity firms
- Bankers
- Recruiters
- Executive recruiters
- Mediators
- Business/CEO coaches
- Life coaches
- Marriage counselors
- Divorce attorneys
- Human resource directors
- HR consultants
- Insurance specialists
- Nutritionists
- Plastic surgeons
- Retirement home/assisted living directors
- Elder law attorneys
- Funeral home directors
- Personal trainers
- Church/religious leaders
- Jewelers

Once you identify a few other types of COIs with whom you would like to build relationships, run an advanced search to find them, then look to get introduced.

Centers of Influence: Your LinkedIn Routine

Building relationships with COIs can be a highly fruitful strategy, but you must be focused in your efforts.

ACTION STEPS TO CONSIDER:

- Review your list of current and potential COIs, and determine which ones you haven't spoken with in a while. Send a message on LinkedIn to stay top of mind. Ideally this is a message adding value, at a minimum it's to touch base.
- Make an effort to like and comment on COIs posts regularly.
- Schedule meetings with your COIs to teach them how to use LinkedIn to grow their own businesses. Share your personal strategy with them.
- On a regular basis, look for people your COIs would find value in meeting. Have a LinkedIn List Sharing meeting to discuss the introductions.
- If you are lacking in the COI category, run an advanced search for COIs in your area. Look for someone who can introduce you to them. If an introduction is not feasible, reach out to them individually and ask for a meeting. Some will be receptive and others will not. It's a numbers game.

CHAPTER **9**

Engaging

There is nothing so annoying as to have two people go right on talking when you're interrupting.

—Mark Twain

If you are overtly focused on self-promotion on social networks, you are driving your connections away. If you are sharing irrelevant content, your connections are becoming numb to your message. Both are damaging your social relationships.

> Michelle was able to figure this out after an initial false start. Her attraction to using social media (in particular LinkedIn) came from her journalism background. Although never a professional journalist, she was a journalism major in college and editor of the school's newspaper. Michelle liked to express herself in writing. She started out by writing only blog posts, and did so far too often. Later, she learned the right combination of posting, engaging, and connecting, which made all the difference.

When most advisors think of their LinkedIn presence, they think about one thing: posting. Don't get us wrong; posting is great. It generates awareness and puts you front and center, right in the middle of your 1st degree connections' newsfeeds. Your connections see your profile photo and the content you are suggesting they review. But posting will only get you so far. Social media is about two-way communication. So let's explore.

3-2-1 LinkedIn Recipe

Your ideal presence on LinkedIn is the right mix of content, engagement, personality, and promotion. It ensures that you're not just pushing content, you are also engaging and humanizing your brand. We've derived the following 3-2-1 formula:

- 3 Parts **Engagement**
- 2 Parts **Content**
- 1 Part **Personal**
- Just a dash of **Promotion**

We call this the 3-2-1 LinkedIn Recipe. In this chapter, we're going to define the ingredients.

3 Parts Engagement

Have you ever been to a social function and encountered someone who was constantly talking about themselves? Every sentence starts with "I" and they respond to your remarks with how they did it *slightly* better, or how their experience upped yours. Did your opinion of this person soar? Did you feel as though you connected?

Why would social media be any different? It's not. Deep down, we know we are our own favorite conversation topics, and all too often our posts on social networking websites reveal this. One of the largest issues we see with advisors using LinkedIn is one-way conversations. You know the type, posts that stand up and scream "me!" and then quietly dissipate into the cyber-void without even a like. Let's rethink this "me, me, me" posting mentality for a second.

You have only a few seconds to grab someone's attention online. As your post appears in their newsfeed, they evaluate who made the post and then read the title. So let's be generous and say you have about three seconds to really hook them. If you haven't established any online rapport, most people will not be listening. As a result, you'll find yourself posting to deaf ears.

In his fantastic book *Likeable Social Media*, Dave Kerpen writes:

> *Listening is the single most important skill in social media, and one that's easy to forget once you get started with all the sexier, more exciting things to do. So whatever you do, once you start, never stop listening. Even once you start talking, it doesn't mean you stop listening—it's quite the opposite actually. ... Results will follow, and it won't be long until your company is the 'coolest person' at the social media cocktail party (and more important, the most successful).[18]*

Nothing will get your 1st degree connections' attention more than listening and engaging them. People crave and track engagement, and it makes them feel good. Spend a few minutes a day reviewing their posts and commenting, liking, and sharing. The more you engage, the more receptive they will become and the more they will actually listen to you. This goes back to being a *Giver*. Give it a try; you'll see what we mean. If compliance is an issue, select non-financial posts and engage with those.

Your comments on others' posts can be as simple as the following:

I read that autobiography too Jen, great book. Love the chapter on . . .

Great post Andy, very helpful!

Thank you! Excellent article on building loyalty with customers. You're right, loyalty is a long-term, earned behavior. It's totally different from satisfaction.

Our research clearly indicates that *Influencers* spend more time engaging with the LinkedIn posts of their connections as compared to non-*Influencers* (Fig. 54). Nearly 80 percent of *Influencers* comment or like posts from their connections.[3]

It's important that you engage with your connections through carefully crafted conversation. Be receptive to their posts and we assure

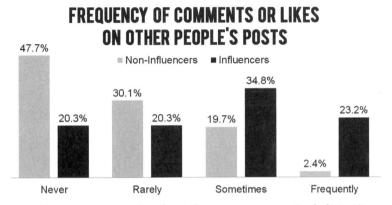

FIGURE 54: Engagement is key for Influencers. Source: Oechsli Institute.

you they will be receptive to yours. Narcissism is a LinkedIn engagement killer.

Signals to Help Nurture Relationships

Michelle held monthly seminars for successful women. Often, prospects would attend her seminars but weren't ready to commit to a formal business relationships at that point. So Michelle would make it her mission to connect with every single one of them on LinkedIn after her event. This gave her multiple opportunities to stay top of mind and engage with them. LinkedIn makes it easy on her to recognize birthdays, work anniversaries, and disseminate pertinent content.

LinkedIn plays a prominent role in Michelle's prospecting process. In her words:

After every seminar I connect with all attendees on LinkedIn. I then message them regularly, send helpful articles, and offer to be a resource—I nurture the relationships. When the moment finally comes and they (or a friend) need financial advice, they think of me first because I've been in constant contact with them. This process takes time, but I bring in far more new clients this way.

Here are ten everyday occurrences on LinkedIn that give you reasons to touch base with prospects and COIs. Think of these as creative points of contact. Used properly, they will help raise overall awareness and progress your relationship. We've also included a few ways you might respond.

1. **They accept your invitation to connect**

   Your Response: *Thanks for connecting with me on LinkedIn and allowing me to be a part of your network. If I can ever introduce you to any of my connections or provide networking support, let me know.*

2. **They view your profile**

   Your Response: *Jim, I noticed you viewed my profile and it reminded me that I needed to reach out to you. It's been a while. We should get together soon.*

3. **They post an interesting status update**

   Your Response: *Great post on [insert topic]. I've always been interested in [insert topic]—keep posting!*

4. **They like or comment on your post**

   Your Response: *Glad you enjoyed it* OR *I always appreciate your insight on my posts.*

   If you notice a prospect or COI consistently engaging with your LinkedIn posts, this is a great time to reach out and schedule a face-to-face interaction. Ask them to lunch or coffee.

5. **They update their profile (e.g., post a new photo, add new skills to their profile, etc.)**

   Your Response: *That's an excellent photo! Where did you get it done?*

6. **They get a new job**

   Your Response: *Congrats on the new job! Can't wait to catch up and hear more about it.*

7. **They have a work anniversary**

   Your Response: *20 years! Wow! That's quite an accomplishment in today's world. Congrats. Let's get back in touch soon.*

8. **They have a birthday**

   Your Response: *Happy birthday! Hope you have a great day.*

9. **They endorse you**

   Your Response: *Just wanted to say thank you for the endorsement. I really appreciate it. Looking forward to reconnecting soon.* OR *Thank you for the endorsement. Unfortunately, due to industry regulations, I am not able to display it on my profile. Regardless, I really appreciate the gesture.*

10. **They connect with someone you know**

    Your Response: *I noticed you recently connected with [Mutual Connection]. I've known [Mutual Connection] for years—great guy. How do you know them?*

> Michelle used most of these touch points regularly, but birthdays and work anniversaries became a personal favorite for her. As for birthdays, she made it a priority to send happy birthday greetings through LinkedIn and at times would send cards or make personal phone calls. She told us, "I can't tell you how amazed prospects seem when I send them a quick happy birthday message. Everyone likes to feel special."

Keep In Touch

LinkedIn's *Keep In Touch* section is an easy way to keep up-to-date regarding your contacts (Fig. 55). This section builds a list of your 1st degree connections who have changed jobs, had a work anniversary, had a birthday, and more. It takes a matter of seconds to review this feature and should quickly become part of your daily regimen.

You can then peruse your lists of connections LinkedIn has created for you, and use these signals as an excuse to reach out (Fig. 56). You can respond directly from this section on LinkedIn. But remember, you don't always have to use LinkedIn to reach out to them. Sometimes

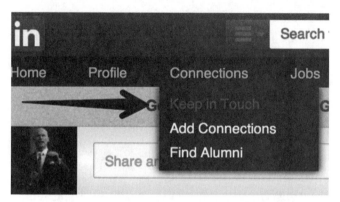

FIGURE 55: The Keep in Touch feature is hidden
under the Connections tab. Source: LinkedIn.

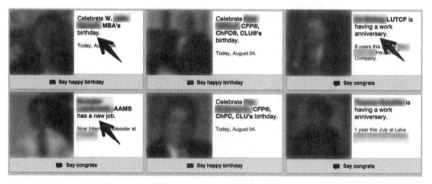

FIGURE 56: Browse your connections for reasons to touch base.
Source: LinkedIn.

shooting them an email or picking up the phone to congratulate them
goes a long way.

Frequency of Engagement

Look to engage with your 1st degree connections' posts on a daily basis.
Be on the lookout for key clients, prospects and COIs. Comment, like,
and share their posts. Show them you are listening.

2 Parts Content

Content is all about posting helpful resources. Because the LinkedIn newsfeed doesn't segment relationships or professions, you aren't just competing against other financial advisors for attention. You are also competing against your connections' colleagues, family members, and friends for attention. With social media, advice is readily available from a multitude of sources. Your goal is to become a new, trusted source for financial advice, and ideally, *the* trusted source.

You must literally give your knowledge away! Yes. You heard us right. Give away everything that you know in small, bite-sized, juicy, content-rich morsels. Doing so will add value to your connections and draw people to you. We know this is a scary thought, but it's the only way to become *the* trusted source.

In his eye-opening book *Youtility*, Jay Baer dives deeper into this concept by recommending you give away content that is so valuable, so helpful, that people would be willing to pay for it. He writes:

> *For your marketing to be so useful that people want it and would gladly pay for it, you have to understand what your prospective customers need to make better decisions, and how you can improve their lives by providing it. . . . The difference between helping and selling is just 2 letters. But those letters make all the difference. Sell something, and you make a customer. Help someone, and you make a customer for life.*[19]

First we have to understand the needs of our prospects, and second we have to create content that is user-friendly and helpful. Consider the following questions as you develop and curate content to post on LinkedIn:

- What are the most common questions asked of you and your staff in real life? Turn answers to those questions into helpful content pieces for LinkedIn.
- Can you help in areas outside of your profession? For example, posting work-stress tips from *Harvard Business Review* can be helpful.

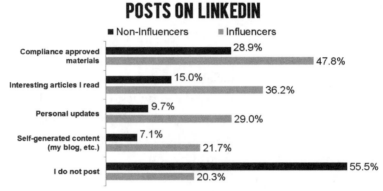

**FIGURE 57: Influencers post a variety of material to their feeds.
Source: Oechsli Institute.**

- How can you listen more and push less? Join conversations and answer questions. Direct your connections to sources for answers.

If you are unable to post right now, don't fret. This stuff is fluid, and we suspect the social media regulatory environment will continue to mature. That said, the *Influencers* who are able to post do find value in it (Fig. 57). They post a mix of compliance-approved materials, interesting articles, personal updates, and more.[3]

Content that Appeals to the Affluent

Regardless of the source, your posts need to be relevant to your connections' interests. If you are trying to identify pertinent topics to post about, look no further than some recent research on the affluent (Table 7). A recent study by Vanguard and Spectrem outlines some of the primary concerns of today's affluent.

Table 7: Primary Concerns of Affluent ($100,000–$1,000,000 Net Worth)[20]	
Maintaining my current financial position	70%
The health of my spouse	65%
My own health	62%
Spending my final years in a care facility	58%
The financial situation of my children and grandchildren	58%
Family health catastrophe	54%
Having someone to care for me in my old age	49%

Source: Vanguard and Spectrem.

Notice a trend? While the number one concern of today's affluent is maintaining their current financial position, most of the other concerns revolve around health and family. This is an opportunity to curate content and create custom content around these topics.

Figure 58 shows an example of an excellent video post from an advisor addressing the number one financial concern from today's affluent. This advisor actually creates custom videos on a number of affluent concerns and uploads them on his website and YouTube channel. He then posts them to LinkedIn. They are typically short, well produced (but not overly produced), and leave the viewer feeling educated.

FIGURE 58: **Great real-world example of a video post. Source: LinkedIn.**

Figure 59 shows another great post from an advisor regarding the importance of having conversations with your family around money.

FIGURE 59: **Real-world post from a financial advisor. Source: LinkedIn.**

It was through a session with one of our LinkedIn coaches that Michelle had one of those "ah-ha" moments. She had fallen into the black hole of posting without a game plan. She was reliving her love of journalism but it wasn't helping her develop her business. She then shifted gears and began to focus on adding posts of interest to her connections, and it made all the difference. To do this, she interviewed her key clients and COIs with whom she was connected on LinkedIn. Perhaps "interview" is too formal of a word to describe the conversation. She really just asked them some iteration of the following:

> Part of our client communication strategy is to provide more value to clients (COIs) we are connected with on social networks like LinkedIn. I wanted to get your insight on what we post and how we can tailor it to you. What are some of your main concerns regarding finances and investments so that we might be able to find or create helpful resources on those topics?

Through simple conversations with clients and COIs, she was able to identify some of their chief concerns and bring more awareness to her LinkedIn strategy. From healthcare to figuring out how much someone needs to retire (their "number"), she created resources that addressed these issues. Once she identified a concern and posted an applicable resource on LinkedIn, she would send the client or COI a direct message through LinkedIn, letting them know the post was for them, and thanking them for the idea. She would also use mentions in her post by typing the @ symbol followed by the person's name in her post. The person she mentioned would get a notification of the post through LinkedIn. The response was always positive and she found her connections were much more likely to engage with her post on LinkedIn if it was made known that the idea originated from them. If the post got more engagement, it was spread to other people outside of Michelle's immediate network.

Michelle discovered that the quality of her posts was extremely important. As she put it, "If I can get my connections to stop and think, laugh, feel inspired, or some other emotion, I'm posting the right content."

Content that Appeals to Your *Ideal Prospect Profile*

Let's take content posting one step further. We know some of the primary concerns of today's affluent in general, but what about the top concerns of those in your network who fit your *Ideal Prospect Profile*?

Refer back to your *Ideal Prospect Profile* (we warned you we would leverage this often) and look for ways to create custom content for them. Envision articles and videos with titles such as:

- *The Top 3 Concerns Raytheon Executives Have about Retirement*
- *How Business Owners Should Approach Personal Healthcare*
- *Helping Merck Executives Save More for Retirement*
- *Lockheed Martin Employees: What You Need to Know About Your Pension*
- *5 Financial Planning Essentials for Engineers*
- *Physicians Need to Plan for Long-Term Care Too*

This type of content is powerful because it's highly targeted. It jumps out and grabs the attention of your prospects. It's customized for them.

Making Your Content Shareable

Now you've developed content that appeals to the *Affluent* and your *Ideal Prospect Profile*. How do you get people to share it?

Getting people to share your content is not an easy task. The amount of information online is daunting, and the number of people posting is booming. We are all becoming media companies, or sources of content (bloggers, vloggers, curators, etc.). So, why is it that some of us post content that gets shared while the rest of us are left scratching our heads? The answer: The content you post needs to be optimized for sharing.

> This probably surprised Michelle as much as anything; her conversational messages, quotes and short videos were shared far more frequently than her mini-editorials she spent hours crafting. She learned that in the digital world, people function in digital time—they want relevant information, and they want to consume it in seconds.

Sharable content is both valuable (relevant and helpful) and snackable (quickly digestible). You can share the most eloquent, insightful content that is so clunky no one wants to take the time to read it. You can also have bite-sized content that just isn't useful. Content that is optimized for sharing avoids both blunders.

Valuable Content

If your content is not relevant to your connections, they find it useless or even annoying. Make sure your content appeals to the affluent and your ideal prospects. If it doesn't answer questions they have, address concerns, provoke emotion, or make them think about their own situations, they probably won't find it of value.

Snackable Content

Less is more. Your connections need to digest your content in a matter of seconds. Take your content and break it up into small chunks. Repurpose your content. If you shoot a video, take quotes from that video and turn them into a series of picture quotes that link to your video.

Consider the following types of bite-sized content:

- **Quotes:** People love to share quotes because they are consumed in a matter of seconds and take no time to vet.
- **Blog Posts:** Keep blog entries around 500 words and highlight your key takeaways. You may want to consider using LinkedIn's publishing platform for blogging.
- **Videos:** Videos that are longer than 60 to 90 seconds are too long. Keep it short and punchy.
- **Pictures:** Include images in your posts because they increase engagement and require little effort to comprehend.
- **Infographics:** Consider using visually appealing and easily understandable infographics instead of full research reports.
- **Articles:** List the highlights or give some personal commentary before posting an article. Make it easy on your connections to decide if it's worth reading or sharing.

Figure 60 is an example of a LinkedIn post that is both valuable and snackable. While this isn't a post about health care, it's valuable in

FIGURE 60:
Like-splosion!
Snackable posts
= engagement.
Source:
LinkedIn.

the sense that it's tied directly to professional development—a big reason a lot of people use LinkedIn. It also combines quotes and images, making it super snackable. Check out the engagement numbers; they speak for themselves. These types of posts are popular and perform well on LinkedIn.

Have you ever received an email that reads more like a short novel? It hits your inbox and you stare at the paragraphs of endless text and wish you could get to the point? Think about the content you share online the same way. You have a few seconds to get to the point. It's a wild content jungle out there. If you don't get to the point, someone else will.

Frequency of Posting Content

Nobody likes constant communication; it becomes numbing and annoying. It's no different than the daily emails you get and ignore. Even if they're on a topic you're interested in, you start to ignore them. Lower frequency is better, but scheduled frequency is best.

Think in terms of posting content three to five times per week. You want to stay top of mind without becoming a bore. Also, LinkedIn has found its most populated times are morning and midday, Monday through Friday. So keep this in mind when you schedule your content posts. If you are taking the time to develop and curate content, you want to be posting when the most people are active.

1 Part Personality

Personality gives a pulse to your professional persona on LinkedIn—it humanizes you. Don't underestimate the value of posts that show your personality. These types of posts share insights into you as a person. Commenting on films, books, music, news, charities, local events and the like, or sharing your know-how on hobbies or interests, can round out a 1st degree connection's image of you, and their propensity to reach out to you for advice.

It's okay to make personal posts on occasion as long as you remain professional. While that seems like contradicting advice—be personal but stay professional—we simply mean keep in mind the culture of LinkedIn. For example, don't post a picture of you partying on your new boat (save that for Facebook). Instead, post pictures from your team's Habitat for Humanity adventure. See the difference?

People love to engage with personal posts. Figure 61 shows a few good examples of advisors showing their personal sides:

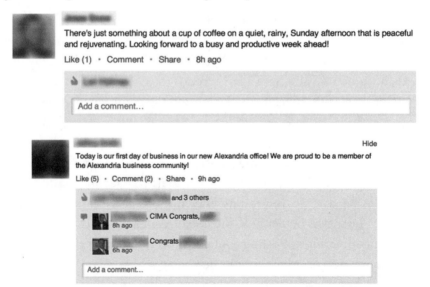

FIGURE 61: Don't be afraid to get personal. Professionally personal, that is.
Source: LinkedIn.

Frequency of Personality Posts

You don't want all of your posts to be funny quotes or personal reflections. After all, you want to be seen as a thought leader for financial services. But personality-based posts do help drive engagement and give insights into you as a person. Look to sprinkle in one or two posts a week that show your personality.

A Dash of Promotion

Promotion is an important part of the communication strategy, but you need to keep blatant promotion to a minimum. Promotional *push* messages are only appropriate when you've developed your 1st degree connections. You've added valuable content, you've engaged with others, sprinkled in some personality, now you are attempting to take the relationship to the next level.

In Gary Vaynerchuk's thought-provoking book *Jab, Jab, Jab, Right Hook,* he reinforces this concept. As Vaynerchuk describes it, "jab, jab, jab, right hook means give, give, give, ask." He suggests that too many people focus on the right hooks and not enough on the jabs. But once you've jabbed enough, you are ready to throw a smashing right hook. Vaynerchuk continues:

> *The emotional connection you build through jabbing pays off on the day you decide to throw the right hook. Remember when you were a kid, and you'd go to your mom and ask her to take you out for an ice-cream cone, or to the video arcade? Nine times out of ten, she said no.*

> *But then, every now and then, out of the blue, she would say yes. Why? In the days or weeks prior, something about how you interacted with your mother before the unexpected outing to the ice-cream shop or arcade made your mom feel like she wanted to do something for you. You made her happy, or maybe even proud, by giving her something she valued, whether it was doing extra chores or good grades or just one day of peace with your sibling. You gave so much that when you finally asked, she was emotionally primed to say yes.*[21]

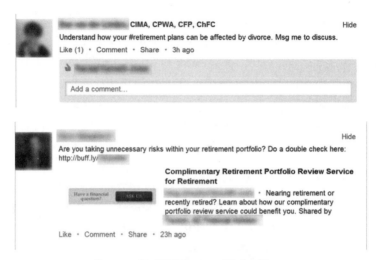

FIGURE 62: KO! Source: LinkedIn.

Vaynerchuk's boxing analogy is brilliant. Your jabs (Content, Engagement, and Personality posts) are designed to build trust, add value, and set up your prospects for your thunderous right hook. Basically, your right hook is when you are asking your prospects to take action—to talk business.

Figure 62 shows a few examples of LinkedIn posts with a promotional tone. Vaynerchuk would refer to these as right hooks.

Make sure you clearly separate right hooks and jabs. There should be no trickery involved. Consistently add value, and when you are ready to throw your right hook, do so with confidence.

Let our 3-2-1 formula serve as a rule of thumb for getting started with your LinkedIn engagement. The ideal formula comes from execution and measurement. Follow it well and you'll jab often enough to land that killer right hook.

Frequency of Promotional Posts

Use these types of posts sparingly. If you are too focused on promotion, your 1st degree connections will become numb to your message. Schedule no more than one or two promotional posts per month.

Who's Viewed Your Profile

We all revel in the thought of someone being interested in us. It doesn't matter if it's online or offline. LinkedIn, unlike most social networks, lets users know who's been looking at their profiles (depending upon their privacy settings). But what do you do when someone checks you out on LinkedIn?

Most advisors do nothing. They receive a notification from LinkedIn or they sporadically navigate to the *Who's Viewed Your Profile* link and start hypothesizing. They peruse the lurkers and conjure up ideas as to why they may have stumbled upon their profiles.

But wait! This is powerful functionality. We're certain that LinkedIn envisioned us using it for much more than an occasional ego boost. It's worth 10 seconds a day to review the *Who's Viewed Your Profile* section. If you want a complete list of who's viewed you, upgrade to the Premium service.

When someone views your profile, the first step is to determine his or her relationship to you. Is it a prospect you've been working on? Is it a client you know well? Everyone has an angle and your job is to uncover it. The second step is to determine how you will respond (if at all).

Some lurkers will almost always warrant a response. Here are a few examples of how you might respond based on the person's relationship to you:

Viewed by Someone You Don't Know

If this is a person you do not know well, but has some prospect or COI potential, you might send a message to connect. In addition, mention your interest to get to know them better. You could say:

Hi JoAnn,

I see we have some mutual connections. It looks like you are in the business of XYZ. I'd love to have a phone conversation at some point in the future if you are open to it.

In the meantime, I would love to connect.

This is not appropriate for each person who views your profile, only for potential COIs or prospects.

Viewed by Someone You Know

If this is a person you are connected to and know well (client, COI, prospect, old friend, etc.), this is a good time to strike up a conversation on LinkedIn. Why? Because you are top-of-mind. You should always nurture your 1st degree connections. You might say:

Hello Jim, hope you are well. I noticed you viewed my profile and it reminded me that we haven't gotten together in a while. When can we grab lunch? Are you free on Friday?

Viewed by a Prospect

If it's a prospect with whom you've already connected, and you notice them checking out your profile, this is a great time to reach out. You can simply place a call (not mentioning that you noticed them viewing your profile) and suggest a social get-together. You might say:

Jim, I know you're a big Brewers fan, I've got tickets for the game this Saturday—can you make it?

The idea is to be "dumb like a fox" and whenever possible, use someone viewing your profile as an opportunity to either develop or strengthen the relationship. There is a reason they are looking at your profile, so the probability of this person responding favorably is much greater when they have done so recently.

Viewed by a Competitor

If the person who's viewing your profile is a competitor, you want to make sure that he or she hasn't been able to sneak by your screening process and become a 1st degree connection. A lot of advisors make the mistake of connecting with too many of their peers and competitors. By the way, your peer today could be a competitor tomorrow. If and when this happens, you should disconnect with this person immediately. If you wouldn't share your client information with them, don't connect with them on LinkedIn.

For those other competitors (2nd degree and 3rd degree connections) checking you out, *c'est la vie*—no response is the best response. Consider this a form of flattery. There isn't anything you can do about it.

These are just some suggestions. The truth is, there is no perfect response. However, neglecting the *Who's Viewed Your Profile* feature altogether is bound to leave some opportunities behind.

Engaging: Your LinkedIn Routine

In this section, we learned a lot about the importance of engagement and posting. Remember, LinkedIn (and social media) is more than just pushing content out.

ACTION STEPS TO CONSIDER:

- Don't just build a connection base—engage them! Review your newsfeed and look for opportunities to comment, like, and share your connections' posts. Look for events on LinkedIn that give you opportunities to touch base with them.
- Respond to all LinkedIn messages in your inbox.
- Check to see if anyone viewed your profile. If they did, review their profile to determine if you want to start a conversation.
- Posting to your newsfeed regularly allows your connections to receive consistent branding and thought-leadership from you. Do this regularly using the 3-2-1 LinkedIn Recipe.
- Acknowledge those who engage with you. If someone comments on an article you post, comment back. Encourage discussion. If this person is someone you would like to meet, reach out after they engage.

CHAPTER 10

Branding

If you're serious about building your personal brand, there will be no time for Wii.

—Gary Vaynerchuk, bestselling author

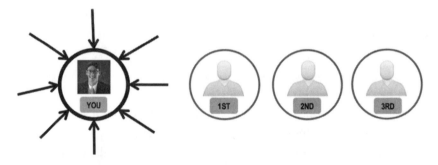

Kathy was convinced that LinkedIn was a waste of time. She was one of the top producers at her firm, living in the Sonoma Valley, and had built her business by cultivating relationships with a handful of high-level attorneys in town. But it was a prospect meeting over a year ago that caused her to change her tune.

The prospect was in his early 30s and had just sold his tech startup business for a lot of money. He was referred to Kathy by a corporate attorney who had helped him with his exit planning strategy. She was excited for the meeting and spent hours preparing.

Before Kathy knew it, the meeting was happening. When the meeting started, everything seemed to be going swimmingly. The prospect answered all of her questions, nodded affirmatively, and gave her all the buying signals she was familiar with. And then, before she knew what happened, everything went downhill. The prospect stopped, looked puzzled and deep in thought and mumbled, "I could find hardly anything about you online, which I thought was odd. I found a lot about your firm, but not you." Kathy didn't know what to say. She was perplexed. Was this really a concern? She felt deflated and proceeded to explain to the prospect, who had just sold his tech business (oops!), that she didn't think an online presence was a top priority.

She was out of touch. We should also mention, she didn't close the business.

The reality is that few *Affluent* investors initially discover their primary financial advisor on LinkedIn. Our research is explicit in telling us that *Affluent* investors select their advisors through personal means. They are personally introduced, meet their advisors though community involvement, or they ask another professional for a recommendation.[9] But, the *Affluent* do conduct copious amounts of secondary research online. As demonstrated in the chart below, the *Affluent* conduct more research online than the non-*Affluent* (Table 8).[1]

Table 8: Affluent Online Search for a Provider (>$500K Investable)		
	Non-Affluent	**Affluent**
Always search online	29%	39%
Occasionally search online	43%	56%
Never search online	28%	5%

Source: Oechsli Institute.

Whether they conduct this research prior to meeting with you or after, it doesn't matter. It creates an impression, and if they conduct this research prior to meeting you, this is literally your first impression.

Once the affluent are officially working with you as their financial advisor, most will want to connect on social media. Surprised? According to a recent study, nearly half of affluent investors want to connect with their primary financial advisor through social media. However, 27 percent of the affluent state they cannot find their primary financial

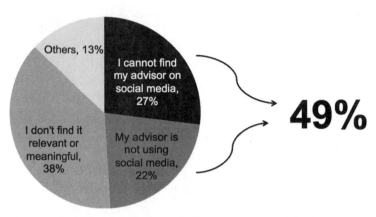

FIGURE 63: Affluent investors' ability to connect with advisors on social media. Source: Finect.

advisor on social media and 22 percent assume their advisor doesn't use social media (Fig. 63).[22] We can expect the demand to connect through social media to continue to grow. If that's the case, you need to make sure your LinkedIn brand tells your story and positions you as the optimal choice. LinkedIn is your professional persona online.

Warning: Before you get started

Before you start making significant changes to your LinkedIn profile, make certain you turn off your activity broadcasts. If you don't, every time you make a change to your LinkedIn profile, LinkedIn will send out an update to your connections' news feeds. This can be annoying, as you are likely to make a lot of changes. To turn this feature off while you make changes, go to *Privacy & Settings* and select *Turn on/off your activity broadcasts.*

We won't go through every single area of your LinkedIn profile. That could be a book in itself. Instead we are going to explore some of the more critical areas.

It's important to design your LinkedIn profile for your clients, COIs, and those who fit your *Ideal Prospect Profile.* Many non-advisor profiles are crafted to attract recruiters. As you encounter these types of profiles, don't feel you have to mimic the way they have developed their LinkedIn brands. Your intent is much different. It's not to brag about the impact you've had for your organization, it's about intriguing prospects to do business with you.

Your Photo

Central to your LinkedIn brand is your profile photo. This is the first thing people will see when they look you up, so taking the time to get it right is well worth the effort. Consumers today research nearly everything online, from the smallest of products to the most expensive service providers. This means your online brand should reflect your real-life brand. Any inconsistency could be a red flag for a potential client or source of connections.

Not having a photo on social networks like LinkedIn can make you seem guarded and antisocial. If you are planning to use LinkedIn for social selling, you must have a photo. According to LinkedIn, profiles with photos get 7 times more views!

Recently, we received a call from an aerospace engineer. He wanted advice on his LinkedIn photo. He said, "I thought it would be a good idea to use a photo of myself with my Harley Davidson in the background. It will show people my passions and that I'm not just an intellect. I'm a real person who likes to ride." Our response: "LinkedIn is a professional network. Your motorcycle in the background might make sense if you worked for Harley Davidson, but not in this case. Get a professional headshot."

It's funny; you wouldn't think we would have to go through this with such a well-educated professional. But the reality is, he has a lot of company. It's important to respect the culture of LinkedIn—it's not Facebook, Instagram, or Twitter.

We thought we'd use the Clint Eastwood spaghetti western title *The Good, the Bad and the Ugly* for this section of the book. It should shed a bit more light on the quality of your photo.

The Good

A good photo can make a great first impression. Here are some commonalities of good photos that we've seen:

- Taken by a professional
- Dress is business or business casual
- Taken from the shoulder up
- Advisor is smiling and looks approachable
- Cropped to the right dimensions
- Has a colorful background to help them stand out in their connections' newsfeed

The Bad

A bad photo can hurt your professional first impression. Here are some photo blunders to avoid:

- Overly and obviously retouched
- Cartoon or caricature
- Blurry, grainy or pixelated
- Your company logo
- Staged photos of you pretending to answer the phone at your desk
- Wedding photo
- Poorly cropped, leaving too much space over the person's head. (This makes them look very short.)
- Obvious that someone was cropped out of the photo. (e.g., ex-wife)
- No photo

The Ugly

You are embarrassing your professional brand by putting these types of photos on your profile. Here are some major photo errors to avoid:

- Selfies
- Webcam photos
- You with a drink or cigarette in your hand (we've seen it!)
- You with your pets

Invest in yourself and each member of your team by hiring a professional to take headshots. People can tell the difference, and you only get one photo—make it count!

Your Headline

By default, LinkedIn populates your *Headline* with your current job title and employer. Most financial advisors don't realize they can edit this. Why customize your *Headline*? The harsh reality is, the only person who really cares about your title is you. Most people couldn't care less about your title; they care about how you can help them. Your *Headline* (that section right under your name) is where you should start demonstrating your value. You have 120 characters and we recommend you use as many of them as possible. You only have a matter of seconds to grab someone's attention online. Without the proper branding and eye-catching language, you can easily be overlooked.

Don't believe us? Imagine you are searching for a financial advisor. You conduct a search and arrive at the following two similar profiles (Fig. 64), and the only difference is the *Headline*. Based on the following *Headlines*, whom would you want to learn more about?

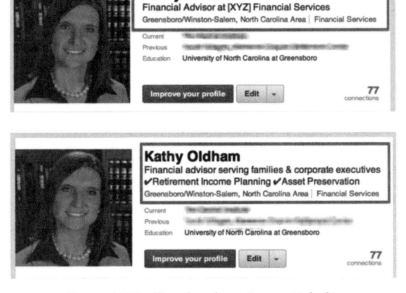

FIGURE 64: Headline showdown. Source: LinkedIn.

Most people are likely to be more intrigued—and certainly more informed—by the second profile. Her *Headline* demonstrates her target market and how she adds value. Because your *Headline* is the first thing people read on your profile, the effort you put into it is well worth it.

There are endless ways to approach crafting your *Headline*. However, try and include a few of the following elements:

- Your searchable title (financial advisor, financial planner, etc.)
- Your value proposition (What do you do?)
- Your target market (Who do you serve best?)
- Your keyword(s) (words you could imagine a prospect searching for)
- Icons to segment sections and standout (e.g., ✔★▶)

Headline Styles

Here are some styles of Headlines you may want to consider. Each has a formula you can use. Pick the one that best suits your personality and business focus.

1. **Declare Your Niche:** This style centers around your niche. Start with a title your target market searches. Next, list the niches you serve.

   Formula: [Searchable Title] | [List of your niches]
   Example: Financial Advisor | Specializing in private wealth management for business owners, executives, and physicians

2. **Question Hook:** This style is an attempt to hook someone into reading your profile and entice him or her to learn more.

   Formula: [Intriguing question] [Value Proposition]

   Example: Need a financial plan? Certified Financial Planner™ helping families make smart decisions with their money

3. **Expert with Proof:** This strategy is to position yourself as an expert but provide some level of proof at the end of your *Head-*

line. Anyone can claim to be an expert—show it by referencing a professional highlight.

Formula: [Proclaim yourself an expert] | [awards, accolades]

Example: Top Financial Advisor in Chicago | Named to Barron's Top 1,000 Advisors

4. **Keyword Heavy:** This style is all about showing up in search results and appealing to a wide variety of people. While it doesn't read well, it includes your keywords that will help drive search results.

   Formula: [Primary keyword] | [keyword] | [keyword] | [keyword]

   Example: Financial Advisor | Houston | Financial Planning | Wealth Management | Estate Planning | 401K

If you feel there is work to be done with your *Headline*, pull up your profile and follow these three simple steps to edit it:

1. Log into your account and select the *Profile* section and hit the *Edit Profile* link.
2. Click on the pencil icon next to *your professional Headline.*
3. Lastly, type your desired *Headline* into the space provided and copy and paste in icons, checkmarks, etc., and hit save.

Your LinkedIn *Headline* is arguably one of the most important parts of your LinkedIn profile (besides your photo of course). People scan your photo and immediately read your *Headline*, so put some effort into it.

Your Summary

The *Summary* section of your profile gives you 2,000 characters to bring your LinkedIn profile to life and tell your story. Similar to your *Headline*, it is an opportunity to color the filter through which the rest of your profile will be viewed. Your *Summary* can be one of the more intimidating components of your LinkedIn profile, and there is no shortage of opinions when it comes to how to write it. The following is a quick formula we've developed and used effectively with many financial advisors.

Summary Guidelines

- Write each section in first person. First-person language gives your profile a natural voice and frees you from the awkwardness of formal third-person writing. Not to mention, writing in third-person on social networks is just weird! (Unless you are a well-known public figure).
- Write for your clients, COIs, and *Ideal Prospect Profile*, not a recruiter or employer.
- Avoid industry jargon, which has a tendency to drain personality from your profile.
- Use keywords to make your profile more search-friendly. However, be sure to use your keywords in a natural manner throughout your *Summary*. Brazenly littering your profile with keywords will only work against you; potentially annoying your reader and making you look sales-y.
- Use bullets when you can.
- Be sure to follow your broker-dealer's policies and procedures (compliance guidelines) for required disclosures.

Summary Template

While keeping the above guidelines in mind, we suggest weaving the five following components into your *Summary*.

1. **Your value proposition:** Start by explaining what you do and how you add value to your clients. What problems do you solve?

2. **Why you do what you do:** Why do you get up every morning to go to work? What motivates you? What do you want to achieve for your clients? What specific event or experience made you choose to become a financial advisor?

3. **Your specialties:** Do you work with a particular niche? Do you solve a specific problem? With whom do you enjoy working? What can people always count on from you?

4. **Something personal:** What do you enjoy doing outside of the office? What are you passionate about? Family? Organizations? Charities?

5. **Reasons to connect:** Conclude or begin your profile with reasons that it may be appropriate for someone to request to connect with you. This is your call to action! What are the situations where your clients need you most? What professionals would benefit from partnering with you? You may want to include an email address associated with your account in this section to make it easier for someone to send you a connection request.

Special Icons

You will notice we also include special icons in the *Summary*. They are designed to simplify sections and catch the eye of the reader. They include symbols such as ✔★▶ .

Note that for this formula to work, you have to make it personal. Give your profile a voice and personality. This is not your resume, but a prospect's or COI's introduction to your unique, professional persona.

Here are a few real-world examples we've helped advisors craft.

Example 1:

I WELCOME A CONNECTION IF YOU ARE:

▶ Seeking a holistic and thoughtful financial advisory team for your family

▶ Interested in an informed second opinion on your financial situation

▶ A corporate executive approaching retirement, recently retired, or experienced a transition

▶ A business owner looking to transition or sell your business

▶ A CPA or Attorney interested in providing a valuable resource for your clients

▶ Tom.Reynolds@XYZWealth.com ☎ 1-800-123-4567

WHY THE REYNOLDS GROUP AT XYZ FIRM?

The Reynolds Group is a leading financial advisory team that works with families, corporate executives, and small business owners to help them prepare a plan for the next phase of their financial lives. The clients we serve typically have a long history of professional success and are now ready to focus on managing their wealth and retirement goals.

TEAM MISSION:

Our advisory team is a resource for the families we serve. We address the following critical financial issues:

★ Portfolio Management

★ Retirement planning and income strategies

★ Philanthropic Services

★ Managing wealth-based risk

★ Trust and Estate Planning Services

DESIGNATIONS:

★ Certified Financial Planner™ (CFP®) certification awarded by the Certified Financial Planner Board of Standards.

★ Certified Investment Management Analyst® (CIMA®) designation, awarded by the Investment Management Consultants Association (IMCA®).

WHEN I'M NOT WORKING:

I enjoy cycling, swimming, golf, and tennis. I support the Make-A-Wish Foundation and Piedmont Wildlife Rehab. My wife Christy and I are trustees of the XYZ Foundation. We live with our son, Leo, in Riverside, California.

Example 2:

ABOUT THE XYZ GROUP:
Our team oversees the financial affairs for a select group of families, retirees, corporate executives, business owners and non-profit organizations in the Triad. We are focused on guiding our clients to achieve their financial objectives with transparency, and a disciplined process. Our guidance is tailored to support our clients' current lifestyle, retirement income needs, and legacy goals, while making them feel comfortable at every step.

SPECIALTIES:
✔ Comprehensive wealth management
✔ Concentrated stock risk management
✔ Retirement accumulation and income-planning strategies
✔ Philanthropic services
✔ Wealth-based risk
✔ Trust and Estate Planning Services
✔ 401Ks

PROFESSIONAL HIGHLIGHTS:
★ Barron's Top 1,200 Financial Advisors
★ Financial Times' inaugural list of top financial advisors

IN THE MEDIA:
I have been a spokesperson for our team in local and national print publications. I am also the host of XYZ Radio Show.

GETTING TO KNOW [FIRST NAME]:
I enjoy Denver's arts scene and serve on the XYZ Board. I am passionate about education and am a supporter of the YMCA.

Media-Rich Links

There is no denying that visual content outperforms non-visual content on social networks. So make your profile stand out from the competition with links to videos, images, documents, SlideShare presentations, and other forms of media that give you an opportunity to enhance your profile and give it an interactive flair.

The ability to add media-rich links to your LinkedIn profile couldn't be easier.

1. Put your profile into edit mode.
2. Scroll down to your *Summary, Experience,* or *Education* sections.
3. Click on the *add media* link. (It's a small blue box in the upper right hand corner.)
4. Add your link or upload a document. If you are adding a link, it must have a public URL address.
5. Now edit the title field and description.
6. Make sure you hit save.

Here are some ideas of the types of rich media links to add to your LinkedIn profile. A couple of these will really make your profile pop.

- An *About Me* or *About our Firm* video
- Videos of any television exposure (news interviews, etc.)
- Links to articles you've written with public URLs
- PDFs of your marketing collateral
- Photos of you receiving awards
- Photos of you giving a presentation in front of a group
- PowerPoint presentations about what you do (upload it to SlideShare).

Also, every time you add a rich media to your profile, it will be broadcast in your connections' newsfeeds and your connections will be able to comment on the new content.

Optimize Your Profile with Keywords

With your branding in place, you are ready to be found, and if you want to be found on LinkedIn, you have to have the right keywords in your profile.

Keywords are not adjectives describing how great you are. *Detailed, professional, experienced* are all great words to fluff up your profile, but they are not keywords. Keywords are terms that your target market uses to search for professionals similar to you. You want to use keywords that are specific to what you do and are terms that people actually search for. Most people don't search for *detailed financial advisor*. Instead, they search for *financial planner charlotte*. This search often takes place on search engines like Google, but LinkedIn results are often some of the first to pop up. Not to mention, more and more people are turning to LinkedIn as a source to find service providers.

Here are a few questions to help you develop a list of keywords to include in your profile.

- What titles do your prospects search for? (Financial Advisor, Financial Planner, Wealth Manager, etc.)
- What services are your prospects looking for? (retirement, financial planning, 401K)
- What certifications do your prospects search for? (CFP, CFA, ChFC, etc.)
- What firm do you work for? Would prospects search for you by firm name? (Merrill Lynch, UBS, Raymond James, etc.)
- What city do you reside in? What city would your prospects use in a search? (Charlotte, Raleigh, Boston, etc.)

Our advice is to have a primary and secondary keyword. Your primary keyword will be a description of your title—*financial advisor, financial planner, wealth manager, wealth management, financial consultant, investment manager*, etc. Your secondary keyword might be another description of your title, a location, or complementary service. For your secondary keyword, consider terms that people might attach to your primary keyword:

- Financial Advisor **Albuquerque**
- Financial Planner **CFP**
- Investment Manager **Estate Planning**
- Financial Advisor **401K**

Once you develop your primary and secondary keywords, your objective is to distribute them throughout the sections of your profile that have the greatest weight for keywords. These sections include your *Headline, Summary, Job Description, Titles,* and *Skills & Expertise.* As you input these keywords within your profile, you want to do it in a natural way. Keyword "stuffing" is looked down upon and can have a negative impact on your brand.

Good Keyword Usage

I've been a <u>financial advisor</u> in Austin, Texas for more than 20 years. I became a <u>financial advisor</u> to help families, corporate executives, and business owners achieve their financial objectives with simplicity, transparency, and a disciplined process.

Bad Keyword Usage

I've always wanted to be a <u>financial advisor</u>. In 1989, I became a <u>financial advisor</u>. I became a <u>financial advisor</u> to help families and small business owners achieve their financial goals. Serving as our client's primary <u>financial advisor</u>, we take a holistic approach. As <u>financial advisors</u>, our passion is fueled by . . .

Putting keywords in your profile is a simple process, but don't go overboard. Also, measure your profile views after you optimize. Are they going up? Down? Then make changes as necessary.

Using LinkedIn's Analytics to Test Your Searchability

Many advisors see LinkedIn as a static webpage. It's simply a place they create a profile and let it forever sit like a modern-day Yellow Pages listing. Alas, these advisors are missing the point. Getting discovered on LinkedIn is a living and breathing commitment, not a "set it and forget it" philosophy (leave that to Ron Popeil). Instead, start thinking of LinkedIn as the new "pay per click" advertisement, a place where you can optimize your professional brand and get found.

LinkedIn's *Who's Viewed Your Profile* section contains some powerful analytics, and more intelligence means better marketing, if you know how to use it. This section is highly visual and easy to understand. Not to mention, LinkedIn even provides helpful tips to optimize your brand at the bottom of the section. Here is a breakdown of how advisors might actually interpret and make use of the data.

Profile Views

This graphic in Figure 65 should look familiar. You should always pay attention to your overall profile views. LinkedIn will graphically show you views from the past 90 days. Here are some tips and questions to keep in mind when viewing this section.

Questions to consider:

- Are profile views trending up or down?
- Are profile views correlated to any other marketing efforts (e.g., eNewsletter blast)?

Actions to consider:

- Complete your profile. According to LinkedIn, users with complete profiles are 40 times more likely to receive opportunities through LinkedIn.

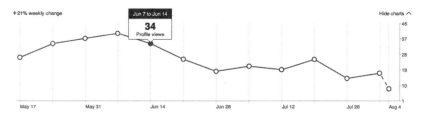

FIGURE 65: The past 90 days of profile activity are automatically charted.
Source: LinkedIn.

- Focus on your photo and *Headline*. If you are showing up in search results (we'll get to that next) but no one is clicking to view your profile, you aren't standing out. According to LinkedIn, just having a profile photo increases page views by 7 times.

Where Your Viewers Work

This section lets you dive into the stats on your viewers' companies (Fig. 66). Hovering over the large *Other Companies* section will give you even more results. Here are a couple of ways to interpret the data and optimize which companies' employees are finding your profile.

152 Other Companies

8 Raymond James Financial Inc.

11 Wells Fargo Advisors

11 Merrill Lynch

13 Edward Jones

Where your viewers work

FIGURE 66: Statistics on where your profile viewers work. Source: LinkedIn.

Questions to consider:

- Are the people viewing your profile associated with companies of clients or COIs you currently work with? If so, investigate further to see if they are connected to any good clients or COIs. (You will need the paid version of LinkedIn to see this).
- If you are unfamiliar with a number of companies from which employees are viewing your profile, you may want to consider investing more time. Perhaps your profile is not optimized for the industry of your target market. For example, if a number of higher education institutions are finding you and you don't work in that market, or have any desire to, you may want to re-evaluate the construction of your profile.

Actions to consider:

- Join groups related to companies in which you would like more exposure.
- Start following companies you would like to target for prospecting or networking opportunities.
- Make sure you connect with anyone you know at companies you are targeting. Especially those with large networks.

Where Your Viewers Live

As an advisor, you probably target a certain geographic location. If that's the case, this next section is critical (Fig. 67). Here are a few ideas to develop a more location-centric profile.

FIGURE 67: Drawing interest from too far abroad won't help much. Source: LinkedIn.

Questions to consider:

- Are the people viewing your profile in close proximity to you?
- Do your profile viewers have a significant affiliation with your local area?

Actions to consider:

- Join location based groups (i.e. Philadelphia Networking Group).
- Include your current location multiple times throughout your profile.
- Connect with all local clients, prospects, and COIs.
- Make sure your location is listed on your profile. If you live in a small town, consider listing a larger nearby location.

Where Your Viewers Came From

This is how your viewers found you (Fig. 68). Perhaps they found you through a LinkedIn search, Google search or group, you get the idea. Also, make sure you hover over the Other Sources section to find additional trends.

125 LinkedIn Mobile App

124 Other Sources

Where your viewers came from

19 People similar to you

25 People You May Know

30 Homepage

FIGURE 68: Analyzing how viewers find you can highlight best and worst sources. Source: LinkedIn.

Questions to consider:

- Are there any clearly underperforming sources? If so, determine how you can stimulate more activity from those sources.
- Are any sources performing well? If so, determine what it is that is helping drive these visitors to your page. Continue putting energy into that initiative, because it's working!

Actions to consider:

- Grow a network that is focused on both quality and quantity. The more high-quality connections you have, the farther your reach.
- Focus on stimulating engagement on LinkedIn. Post relevant content, send personal messages to members, like posts, and acknowledge life events (birthdays, work anniversaries, etc.).
- Make sure you put a link to your LinkedIn profile in your email signature, website, blog, business card, and other social media profiles.

Search Keywords That Led to You

This section helps you determine what keywords are driving profile views (Fig. 69). Specifically, it shows you what sections of your profile are being picked up by keyword searches. As you can see below, some people searched for this individual's first and last name directly, other people found this person by keywords located in their *Summary or job description.*

FIGURE 69: Keyword stats can reveal an underdeveloped profile. Source: LinkedIn.

Questions to consider:

- What keywords do my target clients and COIs use in their searches to find a financial advisor?
- Are people finding me using search terms other than my name? If not, your profile may not be thoroughly completed or optimized with the right keywords.

Actions to consider:

- Select a primary keyword in your profile that your target market might search for. For example, *financial advisor*. Use this keyword naturally throughout your profile, multiple times. The more you incorporate significant keywords, the more boost your profile gets.
- Use variations of similar wording. For example, use *financial advisor* and *wealth manager* and *financial planning*. Sprinkle in these variations.

- *Headline, Summary,* and *Experience* sections should be rich with keywords that your target client searches.
- Include more *Skills* on your profile for desired keywords. LinkedIn lets you choose up to 50 skills—use them. If you aren't, your competition is!

Industries of Your Viewers

This section categorizes your viewers based on their industry (Fig. 70). If you work with professionals from a particular industry, this section is important.

FIGURE 70: Are you hitting your niche? Source: LinkedIn.

Questions to consider:

- Are a lot of financial services professionals creeping on your profile? They may be conducting competitive intelligence, or you may have appeared on a recent webinar for your firm. This also may be an indicator that you are connected to too many advisors.
- Do you work with a niche market but don't see people from that industry viewing your profile? You may need to intensify your efforts with them.

Actions to consider:

- Grow your network with people from your targeted industries.
- Join groups specific to the industries you target.
- Post content that is relevant to your niche.

What Your Viewers Do

This section lists specific job titles of your viewers (Fig. 71).

149 Other Titles

14 Business /
Corporate Strategist

17 Investment
Portfolio Manager

25 Salesperson

69 Financial
Advisor

What your
viewers do

FIGURE 71: **Are execs checking you out? Source: LinkedIn.**

Questions to consider:

- Do your viewers have the job titles you are looking for? For example, are they high-level executives or middle managers?
- Do they have job titles that correspond to the type of professionals you target?

Actions to consider:

- Grow your network with the right types of professionals.

With the paid version of LinkedIn, you can dive into any of these analytics to pinpoint specific people who are viewing your profile. At that point, if you would like to pursue them from a business standpoint, dig into their profiles and look for mutual connections, groups, commonalities, interests, etc. Ideally, there is someone who can introduce you. If there are no commonalities, consider sending them a connection request or *InMail* through LinkedIn.

There are endless ways to interpret the analytics from the updated *Who's Viewed Your Profile* section. We've given you a few thoughts on this topic, but LinkedIn will also suggest ways to help optimize your profile. The most important thing is that you use it! LinkedIn presents your professional brand and gives others the ability to easily find you. It will matter even more in coming years, as the power of social networks evolves—don't let your fear of using these great analytics banish you to obscurity.

Go Public with Your Profile

Once your profile is in good shape, you will want to take it public. Your public profile is what someone sees when they search for you, using a public search engine like Google or Bing. If your profile is not public, the information on your profile won't be indexed by the search engines and people will have a hard time finding you through organic search.

Our recommendation is to make your LinkedIn profile public and all elements visible to everyone. If you insist on your LinkedIn profile being anonymous … don't use LinkedIn! It's like going to a business networking event and not telling people your name or having any business cards handy.

Figure 72 shows how to take your profile public:

1. Select *Profile* at the top of your homepage and select *Edit Profile*.

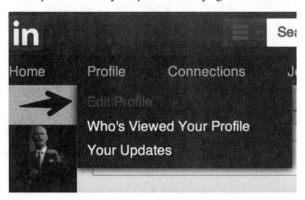

2. Click *Edit* next to the URL under your profile photo. If you have customized your URL with your name (we think you should), it will probably be an address like *www.linkedin.com/in/yourname.*

3. Click the radio button next to *Make my public profile visible to everyone.* Your basic information displays by default.

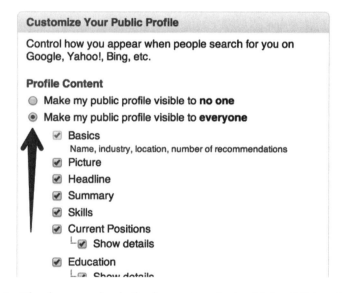

4. Check or uncheck the boxes to select which additional sections you'd like to display. The changes take effect immediately and you'll be able to see them reflected on the page.

FIGURE 72: **Step-by-step description of how to take your profile public. Do it! Source: LinkedIn.**

Branding: Your LinkedIn Routine

Many financial advisors may think of their LinkedIn brand as a one-and-done, but that's really not the case. While you won't need to update your profile every day or week, you should always be building your brand on LinkedIn. Neglect it for too long, and it will soon be outdated—LinkedIn is always adding new features.

ACTION STEPS TO CONSIDER:

- Make sure you have a good LinkedIn photo. Is it out of date? Is it blurry? Unprofessional?
- Ask yourself if there is anything new you can highlight in your profile that will elevate your brand. Any accomplishments? Any new media files? (For example, if you were recognized in the local paper, just got your CFP, or joined your local Rotary.)
- Is your profile optimized for search? It should be!
- Review the *Who's Viewed Your Profile* analytics. Is traffic to your LinkedIn profile increasing or decreasing? Why? Do you need to change your keywords?

CHAPTER 11

Cold Measures

People who read the tabloids deserve to be lied to.

—Jerry Seinfeld

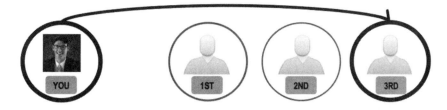

Erik was a new advisor at his firm. He created a LinkedIn account back in college, and it was his prowess using the social network that helped him land his first job in the financial services industry. So it made sense that he would use LinkedIn for prospecting in his new career.

He ran a few advanced searches and created a list of 100 potential prospects and COIs on LinkedIn with whom he wanted to connect. He was participating in our new advisor-training program and asked our opinion on the best way to connect with his newly discovered prospects. Our answer was simple and direct—get introduced! But this wasn't possible for Erik. He had just relocated and his network was sparse. Not to mention, he was under the gun to hit some new asset hurdles.

Out of desperation, he tried everything. He leveraged LinkedIn to send physical letters, emails, *InMails*, cold calls and more. Through a lot of trial and error, Erik figured out what worked and what didn't, and he became a master of cold prospecting using LinkedIn. In a five-month period, he brought in eight new affluent relationships using the cold tactics we are going to teach you.

Most of what we've discussed in this book has been about building a quality network and infiltrating that warm network to gain high-probability introductions. After all, we know introductions are the number one way *Affluent* investors select an advisor. This is our recommended strategy for most financial advisors. But there is more than one way to leverage this powerful social network.

Even if you are not focused on using LinkedIn for colder methods, don't totally disregard this section. While you may not be reaching out to someone cold on a daily basis, there are always times when an introduction isn't feasible. If you stumble upon a prospect outside of your reach, don't be afraid to make use of the tips in this section. This is also the kind of work an intern can handle, with a little guidance.

For some professionals, a colder strategy will be essential. The following types of advisors may be more suited to implement such an approach.

Financial advisors with a limited network

Whether you are a new financial advisor or recently relocated, if your network is limited, a cold strategy may be more suitable.

One of the benefits of building a massive cold network is the perceived credibility it creates. While this may be a game of smoke and mirrors, the perceived credibility can be helpful for advisors who don't have much of a network to start with. For example, if you have a massive network (thousands of connections), when you connect with Mr. Big, now you have numerous people in common. Mr. Big is likely to take notice of all the mutual connections. Hopefully he doesn't ask you how well you know some of those people, but that's beside the point. With a colder strategy, you have to be willing to take these risks.

Another benefit to building a massive network when you're new to the business is scale. Having a network of 6,000 people in your area will help you discover more opportunities. Monitor your network for job changes, promotions, and more. Having a larger network gives you more opportunities to uncover money in motion. And LinkedIn continues to add new features to enable advisors to keep in touch with their networks.

Financial advisors with a highly defined niche

If you have a clearly defined niche, identify your *Ideal Prospect Profile*, find them on LinkedIn, and connect. For example, if your target market is technology startup entrepreneurs in Seattle, connect with as many people who fit this profile as possible. If you primarily work with Air Force officers in St. Louis, connect with as many as possible. You get the idea. Be someone they all know about and think about regularly.

Cold Measures Process

Acquiring new clients using cold measures is a numbers game. Achieving success will take multiple contacts and an array of tactics. Here is the process we coach advisors through when implementing a cold strategy.

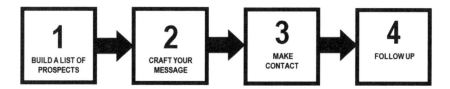

Step 1: Build a List of Prospects

The first step of your LinkedIn cold prospecting campaign is to build a list of prospects. This can easily be done by leveraging the *Advanced Search* feature. If cold measures are going to be an integral part of your LinkedIn marketing strategy, you need to upgrade to the paid version. This will allow you can see more profile information for prospects outside of your network and give you access to *InMails*. Build a list of people who:

1. Fit your *Ideal Prospect Profile*
2. Share multiple commonalities with you (same university, interests, volunteer experience, etc.)
3. Share multiple connections with you

All of these qualifications don't have to be met, but the more you have the more you increase the likelihood of making a connection. With your list in hand, you are ready to craft your message.

Step 2: Craft Your Message

People are busy. If you are inviting someone you have never met to lunch, that's a commitment. If you are asking them for a business meeting, it's an even larger commitment. While these may work at times, we've seen greater success with a message requesting a phone conversation, coffee, or a drink. Your request needs to be non-committal and super-convenient from the prospect's perspective. Also, if you are the one requesting the meeting, you should be the one who is traveling! You should offer to meet at the most convenient place for them (maybe even their office). Let's craft your message.

Write a killer subject line

The first thing your prospect will see is your subject line. It helps them decide to continue reading or ignore the message entirely. Create a subject line that is unique, demonstrates that you've done your homework, and doesn't reek of sales. Your objective is to let the prospect know that you are reaching out to them individually and not sending bulk messages (even though you are). Here are a few examples of subject lines we like.

1. Enjoyed your recent article on [insert topic]
2. Resource for Caterpillar executives
3. Fellow UNC alumni
4. Mutual acquaintance of Trena Horton

Your subject line should be personalized to your target. People can smell a canned message a mile away.

Now that you have your prospect's attention, you are ready to craft the bulk of your message. It needs to come across as authentic and sincere. Here are a few tips.

Acknowledge the cold approach

Start your message by letting your prospect know you've never spoken to them before. While this might seem obvious, it puts the cold nature of the contact front and center. Acknowledging this will help break the ice and position you as an honest person.

Lose the perfect grammar

A message that seems perfectly crafted and punctuated has the risk of looking too much like a template. While you don't want to include blatant misspellings, don't obsess over perfect grammar or being too formal. Use your own language and find your voice in your message.

Less is more

You are basically interrupting someone when sending them a message. So keep your interruption short and sweet. No one wants to read a dissertation.

Make it about them—not you

If your message sounds like it's all about how great you are and what's in it for you, you've missed the mark. Make sure to include at least one or two sentences that demonstrate why it would be valuable for the prospect to speak with you.

Include commonalities and mutual connections

Thoroughly review your prospect's profile before you send your message. Be on the hunt for commonalities. Look at the school they attended, what groups they are a part of, where they've worked in the past, charities/organizations in which they are involved, connections you share, etc. Pick a few commonalities that you can mention in your message to help build rapport faster. It also demonstrates for the prospect that you did your homework.

Have one clear call-to-action (CTA)

Be clear about the next step you are requesting. Don't include multiple CTAs in your message. Here is a classic *bad* example:

> *Would you be open to a brief conversation? If not, do you know other Caterpillar executives who would be open to speaking with us?*

In the above example we are giving the prospect two CTAs when we should be giving one. Drop the referral request. Also, we like using a call-to-action that is easy on the prospect. I could improve my first CTA by saying:

Would you mind if I gave you a quick call this week? I would really appreciate it.

From the prospect's perspective, all they have to do is agree, and sit back and wait for a call.

At first glance, all of these tips might seem like they form an unwieldy message, but that's far from the case. Here are a few examples that use some of the best practices suggested.

Example 1

Subject: Resource for Caterpillar Execs – Fellow U of M Grad.

Tom,

We've never spoken before but I stumbled upon your profile on LinkedIn and wanted to reach out. I noticed we had four connections in common, including John Smith – he's a great guy. I also see we are both Wolverines, Go Blue!

We've helped many similar Caterpillar executives with their retirement and benefit options. No one knows Caterpillar like us! More specifically, we've helped them with things like:

– Retirement accumulation and income planning strategies
– Concentrated stock risk management
– Minimizing taxes

Would you be open to a brief call this week to see if we can be of assistance?

Erik

Example 2

Subject: Congrats on Chronicle article

Hi Tom,

Congratulations on recently being named in the Chronicle – great write up. We've never spoken before, but I wanted to reach out as I noticed that you are not currently working with [XYZ firm]. We provide wealth management services to executives of public and private companies. Given the work we do with your industry peers, I wanted to see if you would be open to scheduling a call with me to discuss some of the ways we work with our clients.

If you have some interest in chatting, is it okay if I give you a call next week?

Thank you, I am looking forward to hearing from you.

Regards,

Erik

Example 3

Subject: Financial Planner for Oracle Executives

Hi Tom,

I know we've never spoken before, but I just read your profile on LinkedIn and wanted to reach out. We manage the personal finances for a number of your colleagues at Oracle like, [insert name]. Also, I visit your office once a month to see clients.

Given the work we do with your industry peers and the fact that I'm going to be in your office next week, are you open to a 15 minute cup of coffee so I can share with you how we work with Oracle executives like you? I would be happy to work around your schedule.

Let me know.

Regards,

Erik

Step 3: Make Contact

With your message in hand, you are ready to make the *O-2-O Conversion*™ happen. There are multiple mediums you can leverage to make contact with your prospects. We recommend a combination of the following as they are not mutually exclusive.

1. **Cold Connect:** This method involves sending a cold invitation to connect on LinkedIn first. Once your prospect accepts your invitation to connect, you can send them a direct message through LinkedIn.
2. ***InMails:*** *InMails* are messages to LinkedIn users who are outside of your network. This is one of the reasons you need a premium (paid) version of LinkedIn.
3. **Emails:** This tactic will require you to uncover the email address of your prospect.

Let's explore each of these tactics.

1. Cold Connect

Most social media experts will tell you that requesting to connect on LinkedIn without ever meeting the prospect is heresy. Not to mention, you are going against LinkedIn's internal policies. However, there are always exceptions. If you are a new advisor with hurdles on the horizon, or recently relocated, this is a risk worth taking.

The first step for using this method is connecting to your prospect. Once you are connected, you can send them a direct message through LinkedIn. We recommend waking up every morning and sending connection requests to 10 potential prospects. Here are a few tips to help you craft an effective cold connection request on LinkedIn. You must make a genuine and compelling argument for connecting.

Personalize!

If you were planning to use the standard *I'd like to add you to my professional network on LinkedIn,* please reconsider. It's going to take considerably more time to personalize each connection request, but we guarantee that more people will accept your request to connect if it's personalized. Write a well thought-out and personal invitation to connect. You might say:

> *Tom, I saw on LinkedIn that you're a member of the Chamber of Commerce, I'm new to town and . . .*

Mention a Commonality

The information is out there, so use it! Peruse the target's profile and be on the hunt for anything you can reference as a commonality. This is important. This might be as simple as referencing a school you both attended, a group you share, or an organization you both support. Also, look through other social networks and conduct a Google search on them and see what you find. If you find information that would be perceived as public knowledge, use it. For example, if they were referenced in a local paper, make note of it. Show that you've done your homework.

> *Tom, I saw you were recognized in the News & Record for your involvement with Make-A-Wish—I commend your work. I am actively involved in . . .*

Reference Relationships

If you have mutual connections make sure you reference them in your request to connect.

> *I see we have some mutual connections on LinkedIn, including Jason Lemus and Lindsay Dawn.*

Stroke Their Ego

Don't be manipulative or over the top, but do make them feel good. This can be as simple as acknowledging an award that was listed on their LinkedIn profile. Maybe it's referencing them as "successful" or telling them they have a "great profile." You get the point, be subtle.

> *Tom, congratulations on your promotion to VP Regional Manager at VF Corp . . .*

Be Concise

You only have 300 characters to personalize your request. You have to keep it as concise as possible. This might mean picking and choosing what you include. Notice that our example below is fairly brief.

Have One Clear Call-to-Action (CTA)

Your only request when cold connecting is to connect, period. Requesting to connect *and* suggesting a phone conversation might be a bit overwhelming for some prospects. Keep this simple.

I'd like to add you to my network.

Here's how your message might look, by combining some of the points above.

Tom,

I saw we are both U of M grads and both of us are connected to Stephen Boswell. I found you on LinkedIn while looking for business owners in [location].

I'd love to add you to my network. Go Blue!

—Erik

When your prospect accepts your invitation to connect, use the message we crafted in step 2 to request a conversation. Because you are now "connected" on LinkedIn, you can send them a direct message through LinkedIn.

Can "cold connecting" really be the new cold calling? It's not far removed from it. Just approach it with similar expectations. It's a gutsy approach. Just don't let *gutsy* turn into *annoying*. Your first invitation to connect is really about generating awareness. It's still going to take time to win their trust and business.

WARNING! At the time of this writing, if you get five *I don't know* (or *report spam*) responses from invitations you've sent to connect, your account becomes restricted. This means that any future invitations you send out will require that you know the person's email address. This first offense is really a hand slap. You can make an appeal to LinkedIn and they will reinstate your account.

2. InMails

If cold connecting isn't your cup of tea, you can also send an *InMail*. *InMails* are like direct emails through LinkedIn to people with whom you are not connected. Some people refer to them as the "Hail Mary Pass" of LinkedIn messages. They are an excellent way to reach people outside of your network and according to LinkedIn, they are 30 percent more effective than standard emails. But *InMails* are not free. Again, this is why it's important to upgrade to a paid account to take full advantage of them. *InMails* are guaranteed a response by LinkedIn. If you don't get a response, LinkedIn will credit you back your *InMail*.

Crafting an *InMail* that gets a response is an art. You are still reaching out cold. Think of them as conversation starters, not sales pitches. It's better to send 20 well-crafted *InMails* than 100 poor ones, hands down.

Before you send an *InMail* to someone, determine if they are an active user on LinkedIn. You don't want to waste your *InMails* on prospects who rarely check their LinkedIn profile. Review the prospect's profile and ask yourself the following:

- Do they have a profile photo, *Headline*, and *Summary*?
- Do they have more than 50 connections?
- Do they use the paid version of LinkedIn?

If you answered affirmatively to any of the previous questions, you should proceed with sending your *InMail*. If not, consider saving it. It may take a while for this person to ever see your *InMail* in the first place.

3. Emails

You can also send prospects your message via email. With emails, you won't be limited to using a finite number of messages like *InMails*. But the challenge will be uncovering their email address. Here are a few tips:

Review their LinkedIn Profile

Some people list email addresses on their LinkedIn profiles. Make sure you check this first.

Company Website

If your prospect works for a small to medium-sized business, key members of the team may be listed on the website with contact information. Check that next.

Figure Out the Email Formula

If you cannot find your prospect's email address on their LinkedIn profile or company website, try conducting a Google search to figure out the company's email "recipe." Most email addresses use a common formula. For example, if I were trying to determine the email address for my prospect Tom Reynolds, there is a good chance it's one of the following:

- Thomas.Reynolds@XYZ.com
- Tom.Reyolds@XYZ.com
- Tom_Reynolds@XYZ.com
- TomReynolds@XYZ.com
- TReynolds@XYZ.com
- Tom@XYZ.com

A Google search can help you figure out the formula. You might input the following into a Google search: "*email: * @XYZ.com*". The asterisk is a wildcard. This means that Google can fill in the blanks. Google will attempt to find emails that end with @XYZ.com and you will be able to see examples of the formula the company uses.

Another great website you can leverage to figure out email formulas is email-format.com.

Lastly, an excellent service to help you figure out and verify emails is MailTester.com. It's a free service that allows you to input and verify any email address.

Once you determine the email address of your prospect, you can send them the message you crafted in step 2.

Step 4: Follow Up

If you don't get a response to your first message—send another. We've found that many advisors who do this get a better response rate the second, third, or fourth time around. After five to seven days, send a similar message as a follow up to your initial message. In this message, acknowledge that you have messaged them in the past and get specific with your call to action. For example:

Tom,

I sent you a message a few days ago, but wanted to reach out once more. We oversee the financial affairs for many executives at Caterpillar and have helped them with XYZ.

Would you mind if I called you sometime this week for 10 minutes?

Please let me know.

Erik

When done properly, cold prospecting techniques can be extremely effective. The secret lies in the personalization. Too many people on LinkedIn send messages that scream *copy and paste.* Spend some time personalizing the message and clearly demonstrate your value for the prospect or COI.

Cold Measures: Your LinkedIn Routine

If you are using LinkedIn for cold prospecting, you will need to put consistency behind your approach. After all, cold prospecting is a high numbers game.

ACTION STEPS TO CONSIDER:

- Build a list of prospects using LinkedIn's *Advanced Search.* Try and identify prospects with whom you share commonalities and connections.
- Cold Connecting: Invite a handful of prospects to connect every day. Make sure you personalize your request using the tips and techniques in this section. Once you're connected, build rapport and then request a real world conversation.
- *InMails*/Emails: Unless you are paying for the highest level of LinkedIn, you probably won't be able to send *InMails* every day. That said, spend a few minutes each day searching for prospects you would want to contact and if you find one, send them the "Hail Mary Pass" message. Remember, you can also use email.

CHAPTER 12

Relationship Management

Always borrow money from a pessimist. He won't expect it back.

—Oscar Wilde, writer and poet

Jim was great at using LinkedIn intelligence. He had become extremely proficient at connecting with clients, prospects, and COIs, and using the information he gathered through LinkedIn to deepen relationships. As he put it, "Rapport is power. There is so much information on LinkedIn that I can use in conversations." I always start there with any new relationship.

Develop Rapport Faster

It's okay to be a stalker on LinkedIn. We say that jokingly, kind of. If you were to congratulate a prospect on breaking their high school record for the 100-yard dash because you found it on the fifth page of a Google search, they may start running for the hills. People might start thinking you work for the NSA, or calling you The Googler behind your back. Even though it's public knowledge, it can come across as invasive. But if you were to tell a prospect you reviewed their LinkedIn profile before meeting, it would seem thorough, not creepy. Why? The culture of LinkedIn. It is understood that people are on LinkedIn for business purposes and everyone has opted in.

Make a habit of profiling people on LinkedIn before face-to-face meetings. When used correctly, the information available online can help you develop rapport at an accelerated pace.

> After scheduling a lunch with a CPA he was targeting as a potential referral alliance partner, Jim spent 15 minutes profiling his upcoming lunch date. He quickly discovered that this CPA was very involved in an organization called Food Assistance, a local organization that delivers groceries to the elderly. Using the information he gathered, much of the discussion revolved around Food Assistance.
>
> Although Jim's overall objective was to develop a referral alliance partner, he left that lunch meeting with a social follow-up game plan. Jim and his spouse, along with CPA and his spouse, were going to attend a local theater show where all proceeds went to Food Assistance.
>
> Jim began to build a personal relationship with this CPA and six months later he received his first affluent referral from this CPA. As of this writing, it's been nearly a year and Jim has brought on four new affluent clients directly from this CPA.

Before each prospect meeting or social function, look up key attendees' profiles on LinkedIn. Think about how you can weave the information they share into conversation, or use it to seed questions. In particular, look for commonalities among the following, as they are the easiest to bring up in conversation and can give you instant credibility.

Connections you share
Look to see if you share mutual connections, especially those who seem to be on the same level as your prospect. For example, if you are meeting a CEO, look for other CEOs you both know.

Schools you both attended

If you attended the same university, this is great to bring up. If you didn't attend the same *alma mater*, do you know someone who did attend that university around the same time period? Do you know about that school's sports teams or special events? What is that university known for?

Groups or organizations in which you are both involved

If you are both involved with the same nonprofit or concerned about a similar cause, use this to help build rapport.

Hobbies you both enjoy

This is something to mention if you truly share the same passion. If you start talking to them about golf because you noticed it on their LinkedIn profile, and they ask you about your handicap and you don't know what that means, you lose credibility.

Places you both grew up

If your hometowns are in the same region, bring it up. For example, if you both grew up in San Diego, you can instantly bond over the amazing Mexican food and the Gaslamp district.

Places you both have worked

If you've both worked at the same company, you definitely want to bring this up. If you haven't, but know someone you feel was credible at that company, mention them. There's a decent chance they know each other.

Using this information is an art form. A simple question can put the information into play: "I noticed from your LinkedIn profile that you like to ski. Where is your favorite place to go?" Don't barrage your prospect with a bevy of questions culled from their profile; if you have other interests in common, weave the information into the dialogue naturally. If it seems like you've memorized their LinkedIn profile, you will only come across as creepy.

Also, you need to be sincere. Don't pretend to be interested in something you discovered on their LinkedIn profile if you aren't. This can come across as extremely disingenuous and hurt your credibility.

> Jim's budding relationship with the CPA prompted him to develop the habit of profiling every prospect, COI, and power player at social functions. Invariably, it helps him to establish rapport and frequently leads to a second point of social contact. As Jim put it, "The last fundraiser I attended resulted in two social follow ups—a round of golf and a sailing trip. LinkedIn profiling gave me the ammunition, whereas before, I would have attended without doing any homework and it would have been more difficult to come up with follow-up ideas. Now I enter into every social function with follow up ideas based on information I've gathered from their LinkedIn profile ahead of time."

Once we're able to get advisors into the habit of doing their homework (profiling relationships online), it doesn't take long for them to come to the realization that this exercise is a relationship accelerator. It enables them to strengthen bonds with existing clients and rapidly develop new relationships with referral alliance partners and prospects.

Relationship & Contact Info Tabs

Unless you are totally asleep, you've probably noticed that LinkedIn is looking more and more like a customer relationship management (CRM) system. The amount of information on LinkedIn is insurmountable. What's so perfect about all of this is that the information is self-proclaimed. You know it's accurate, at least it was at the time it was entered. Here's what's even better though, you can *add* information about each of your contacts that is only visible to you.

By utilizing the *Relationship* and *Contact Info* tabs, you can add notes, reminders, and tag your contacts.

Relationship Tab

With the *Relationship Tab,* you can type in notes about each of your best contacts (Fig. 73). We've seen advisors type in names of prospects they want their connection to introduce them to in this section. You can also set reminders to reach out to them. This is perfect for that CPA you need to reach out to every month. You can actually set recurring reminders!

FIGURE 73: The Relationships tab is a killer way to keep notes on connections. Source: LinkedIn.

You can also keep notes on how you met and tag the connection. It's a good idea to tag clients, prospects, CPAs, attorneys, and more. This will help you find them faster and you can send customized messages to each segment later.

Contact Info

The *Contact Info* section is great for storing information that you find most helpful for each connection (Fig. 74). Some of their contact information is pre-populated—that's great. But if it isn't, you can add additional details to this section. Perhaps you know their cell phone number but they don't list it on their profile. If that's the case, you can enter it here.

FIGURE 74: Use the Contact Info tab to flesh out information left out of public profiles. Source: LinkedIn.

These sections are helpful for staying on top of your best LinkedIn relationships. Just remember, the information you enter into the *Relationship* and *Contact Info* sections are only visible to you.

Surprise and Delight Clients, Prospects, and COIs

LinkedIn does a good job of informing you about your connections' birthdays, job promotions, job anniversaries, and job changes. In addition, LinkedIn profiles are full of personal information that gives you insight into your connections' passions. You can use this intelligence to 'wow' your connections and position yourself as a *Giver*.

If you have a strong enough relationship with your connection, you might consider sending them a small, thoughtful gift from time to time. We refer to these as surprise and delight touches. For example, if your client is a member of the LinkedIn Duke Alumni group, a college sweatshirt or basketball schedule might be a nice personal touch. It would be a "surprise" and cause a bit of "delight"—hence the label.

For instance, LinkedIn notified Jim that his new CPA partner had a birthday. He sent a bottle of his favorite wine to the CPA's home in addition to giving him a personal call. By the way, birthday *calls* are more personal and have more impact than birthday *cards*.

From time to time, Jim received notifications that prospects were either promoted or had a birthday. In these situations, a bottle of wine would be over the top, but a Starbucks gift card or an eCard would be in order. Jim was building emotional equity with his connections by surprising and delighting them. This really got people talking. When he first started the idea he was a bit skeptical. But he quickly realized the buzz it created was well worth the effort. He can attribute multiple new clients from the positive word of mouth that spread from these thoughtful gestures.

Relationship Management: Your LinkedIn Routine

LinkedIn is great for uncovering information to help you develop rapport faster, and position yourself as a Giver.

ACTION STEPS TO CONSIDER:

- Review LinkedIn profiles before upcoming client, prospect, and COI meetings. Use this information to develop rapport-building questions.
- Use LinkedIn intelligence to come up with Surprise-and-Delight gift ideas.

CHAPTER 13

Your 30-Minute LinkedIn Routine

I love deadlines. I like the whooshing sound they make as they fly by.

—Douglas Adams, author of
Hitchhiker's Guide to the Galaxy

There is an inevitable question asked by our social media clients: "What should I be doing on LinkedIn every day?" Simple question, right? The truth is, you have better things to do than spend all day on LinkedIn. However, if you are efficient with your time you can benefit from LinkedIn without it turning into a time-sucking black hole. You know the feeling—you putz around on LinkedIn for a while, before you know it, way too much time has passed and you feel like you've accomplished nothing.

The good news is we've been building your LinkedIn routine throughout this book, and have compiled it into an easy list for you to review. Ideally, you can get it down to a 30-minute daily regimen. Below is a list of possible activities—many were included at the end of each chapter. We segmented them by daily, weekly, monthly, and occasional actions. That said, the frequency is not set in stone. Some activities can be done more or less based on your desire to grow. For example, we put *Requesting an Introduction* in the weekly checklist, but you can easily (and probably should) request two or three introductions a week. You will need to determine the optimal frequency of some activities.

Lastly, for the sake of simplicity, we omitted actions for advisors who moderate their own groups or are taking a cold prospecting approach.

Daily Actions
Respond to messages/invites in your LinkedIn *Inbox*
Review your newsfeed and engage (comment, like, share)
Check discussions in your top 3–5 groups and engage
Find a new connection (*People You May Know*, people you've met, etc.)
Post a status update with helpful content (3–5 times a week)
Review *Keep in Touch* for birthdays, work anniversaries, new jobs, etc.
Review *Who's Viewed Your Profile*
Find someone who fits your *Ideal Prospect Profile*
Review LinkedIn profiles of upcoming client, prospect, and COI meetings

Weekly Actions
Request an introduction
Touch base with a *Connector*
Position yourself as a *Giver* to a client, COI, or *Connector*
Review the results of your saved searches
Conduct a Connection's Connection search for prospects
Post an update that shows personality
Post helpful content within your top 3-5 groups
Touch base with a dormant connection
Get more personal with a superficial connection
Search for your *Ideal Prospect Profile* in a group directory

Monthly Actions
Conduct advanced search for non-saved searches
Conduct a LinkedIn List Sharing meeting with a COI
Conduct an educational meeting around LinkedIn with a COI
Uncover a Surprise and Delight idea from a connection's profile

Occasional Actions
Review your profile and determine any updates needed
Review *Who's Viewed Your Profile* analytics
Post a promotional update

There are obviously many other things you can do on LinkedIn, but this is a great starting point. At first, this routine may take a little longer than 30 minutes, but once you get into the rhythm, it will be much quicker to complete.

Staying Current

Since we began writing this book some 12 months ago, a lot of changes have taken place. This is the reality of social media, or as many would say, the new normal. It's with this understanding that we've attempted to provide you with both a working knowledge of what's currently available through LinkedIn, and a process for taking advantage of this powerful tool. Our objective isn't to transform you into a social media or LinkedIn expert. Hardly. The sole purpose of this project is to help accelerate your business development, with LinkedIn now being one of your powerful tools.

Regardless of new developments, whether it's new social media outlets, enhancements to LinkedIn, or FINRA's regulatory guidelines, the *O-2-O Conversion*™ is likely to remain a key ingredient to your success in acquiring affluent clients. Our ongoing *Affluent* research goes far beyond social media and LinkedIn. For the past decade, word-of-mouth influence and personal introductions have been the primary influencers in *Affluent* major purchase decisions. We don't expect to see this change as social media continues to gain mainstream acceptance in affluent circles.

That said, it's fairly easy to stay current without getting lost in the black hole of social media. All you need to do is follow the right people, and periodically read the right blogs and resources. You can do this yourself, delegate it to a team member, or even put your intern in charge.

The idea is to stay connected to sources that will send you messages, alerts, and more related to LinkedIn, FINRA, and new social media advances. Below is a listing of how you can keep in touch with us, as well as some of our favorite social media and financial services experts. Some of these links may change over time—that's okay. Just run a Google search to find the updated links. There are endless social media "experts" out there. Just make sure the other sources you follow are credible and the people you read about are true experts in the industry.

Shameless Plugs:

- Follow @MattOechsli, @KevinANichols and @StephenBoswell. We're constantly posting new social selling techniques and ideas and ways to sell to the affluent.
- Join the Oechsli Institute's LinkedIn group and engage with us!
- Visit our website and blog https://www.oechsli.com/

A Few of Our Favorite Social Media Experts:

- Follow @KokaSexton. He's the Senior Social Media marketing manager for LinkedIn and a thought leader on social selling. He also has a great blog: http://www.kokasexton.com/word/
- Follow @GaryVaynerchuk and read his blog: http://gary vaynerchuk.com/blog/ The work of social media doesn't get more exciting than Gary!
- Follow @DaveKerpen and read his blog: http://www.davekerpen. com/blog.

- Follow @JayBaer and check out his website: http://jaybaer.com/
- Follow @ChrisBrogran and check out his blog: http://chrisbrogan.com/blog/

A Couple of our Favorite Financial Services Experts:

- Follow @MichaelKitces. He's a financial planner, blogger, speaker, and educator. Read his well-known blog Nerd's Eye View: http://www.kitces.com/blog/
- Follow @BillWinterberg. He's the go-to guy in the financial services space when it comes to technology. Also, make sure you check out his video blog Bits and Bytes: http://fppad.com/blog/.

Regulatory Restrictions:

- Go to http://www.finra.org/ and search social media for the most up-to-date rules and filings.
- Visit http://www.sec.gov/news/socialmedia.shtml

Mastering LinkedIn should be fun, as well as profitable. So enjoy yourself as you learn the ins and outs of using LinkedIn as a sales tool. Yes, LinkedIn is just a tool. But it is a powerful tool when in the hands of a financial advisor who has taken the time to master its power. Commit yourself to apply what you've learned in these chapters, as it applies to you, and watch the results unfold.

Connect, build relationships, stay current, and keep executing the *O-2-O Conversion™.*

Sources

1. "Affluent Purchasing Decisions Report." *Oechsli Institute* (2014): n=658

2. "Elite Advisor Report." *Oechsli Institute* (2014), n=424

3. "Financial Advisor Social Media Survey." *Oechsli Institute* (2014) n=917

4. "MLC Customer Purchase Research Survey." *Corporate Executive Board* (2011).

5. "Why Are Seniors the Fastest Growing Demographic on Social Media?" Narr. Melissa Block. *All Things Considered. NPR.* Natl. Public Radio. Web. 25 November 2013. <http://www.npr.org/templates/story/story.php?storyId=247220424>

6. "Influencing the Mass Affluent." *LinkedIn and Cogent Research* (2013): n=502

7. "Financial Advisor Social Media Survey." *Oechsli Institute* (2012): n=649

8. "Your Network and Degrees of Connection." *LinkedIn Help Center.* LinkedIn Corporation, n.d. Web. <http://help.linkedin.com/app/answers/detail/a_id/110/~/your-network-and-degrees-of-connection>

9. "Affluent Investor Study." *Oechsli Institute* (2014): n= 751

10. Grant, Adam. *Give and Take.* New York: Penguin, 2013. 40-41

11. Vaynerchuk, Gary. "The Secret to Networking? Leverage." *Wall Street Journal: The Accelerators* 17 March 2014. Web. <http://blogs.wsj.com/accelerators/2014/03/17/gary-vaynerchuk-the-secret-to-networking-leverage/ >

12. Gladwell, Malcolm. *The Tipping Point.* New York: Little, Brown and Company, 2000.

13. "Financial Advisor Social Media Survey." *Oechsli Institute* (2013)

14. "Removing a Connection." *LinkedIn Help Center*. LinkedIn Corporation, n.d. Web. <http://help.linkedin.com/app/answers/detail/a_id/49/~/removing-a-connection>

15. Dunbar, Robin. *How Many Friends Does One Person Need?: Dunbar's Number and Other Evolutionary Quirks*. London: Faber and Faber, 2010.

16. "Employment and Training Administration Fact Sheet." *US Department of Labor ETA*. US Department of Labor, n.d. Web. <http://www.doleta.gov/programs/factsht/warn.htm>

17. DHR International and Modern Survey, 2013

18. Kerpen, Dave. *Likeable Social Media*. New York: McGraw-Hill, 2013. 24

19. Baer, Jay. *Youtility: Why Smart Marketing is About Help not Hype*. New York: Penguin, 2013. 121

20. "Today's Affluent Investor: Insights and Opportunities." *Vanguard and Spectrem Group* (2013): 16 .

21. Vaynerchuk, Gary. *Jab, Jab, Jab, Right Hook*. New York: Harper-Collins, 2013.

22. "Financial Advisor Social Media Study." *Finect* (2013)

Index